A. J. King is 57 years old and an artist, coach and author living in Scotland. In 2009 she experienced a series of unfortunate events that would test the strongest person. She survived and learned lessons that would set her up for a dramatic turnaround. Making her story into a work of fiction was the only way she could tell it.

This is the first of two books that will share her story of losing everything only to eventually find her holy grail.

Her artwork depicts women and their power and her website showcases all of her creative works and her powerful new signature coaching programme 'The Creative Business Academy.'

Find her at www.mandynicholson.co.uk

To my children Becca and Dan who are my inspiration.

A. J. King

THE LIFE I WON

An Inspirational Story About What Really Matters When You Lose Everything

AUSTIN MACAULEY PUBLISHERS™

LONDON ∗ CAMBRIDGE ∗ NEW YORK ∗ SHARJAH

A CIP catalogue record for this title is available from the British Library.

ISBN 9781398413559 (Paperback)
ISBN 9781398413566 (Hardback)
ISBN 9781398405103 (ePub e-book)
ISBN 9781398413573 (Audiobook)

www.austinmacauley.com

First Published 2022
Austin Macauley Publishers Ltd®
1 Canada Square
Canary Wharf
London
E14 5AA

I would like to acknowledge my husband, Gary, and my two children Becca and Dan for putting up with me in writing this book in our living space. It won't be long now until we are in our dream home, in fact when this book is published, we will be firmly in place!

I would like to acknowledge my sister and my mum, who have always been a huge part of my life even at the worst of times and I am happy to say that my sister and I have a fantastic relationship these days.

To my good friend Naomi who was my saving grace at times, and my "Irish liqueur" drinking partner. Also, my best friend Louise who was at the other end of the country and I never told how bad things were because she had her own problems, but I have honoured her by using her name and picking out her "Scottishness" in Naomi's character.

Finally:

To my dad, who taught me so much. You are remembered every single day with love.

Table of Contents

Chapter 1
Fourth of March 2009 – Crash

As Mandy King awoke that morning, she knew that today was going to be another battle. Outside it was gloomy, the air was thick and when she emerged from her crumpled bed before the alarm even signalled 5 a.m. every single step felt sluggish. There were way too many 5 a.m.'s in her working week. However, start the day she must. Being the main breadwinner, responsibility weighed heavy on her to provide for her family, but she couldn't help wondering how life had gone from facing every day with excitement and anticipation to dreading it.

What seemed like yesterday, Mandy was flying high in a career that she had seemed to just fall into and enjoyed every second of. As a successful top executive in her company, she had broken through the misogyny and put female managers firmly in the picture. Never afraid to take on a challenge, and embracing every problem as an opportunity she had been a well-respected role model and change maker.

Headhunted twice by global companies she was really making a mark and earning a six-figure package. Every day had felt like an adventure and the alarm clock was an unnecessary tool replaced by adrenaline, expectation and achievement. Driving her onwards and upwards was her natural-born talent as a leader, motivating and inspiring others with ease and with charisma in abundance.

So why, on this dreary, dark and ominous morning did she feel like she had nothing to keep going for?

It was so unlike her to feel this way, her usual mindset was positive, forward-thinking and filled with gratitude for all that she had achieved. Her two beautiful children were her pride and joy and she was lucky enough to have her husband at home so that they didn't have to consider placing her precious cargo into childcare. They lived in a stunning remote farmhouse with views that could have been painted by Turner and had two dogs who brought real joy to them. She had it all.

But today, gratitude seemed a long way away. Sometimes the fog feels too thick, but why?

Oh well, she thought, *just get up and do it anyway.* So, after a hot shower and a large coffee, Mandy kissed the children tenderly on their foreheads, walked the dogs and slumped into her car to make the hour-long commute to work.

Normally she took in the natural beauty that surrounded her on her route to the motorway, however, today the trees seemed mocking and the sheep had turned their backs. The usual racing hares and frisky rabbits were in hiding and even the cows seemed to be at the far side of the fields. The whole world seemed to be shunning her in such an obvious way, or was this all in her head? Why was her thinking so negative? Why could she not see the beauty or feel the gratitude today? What on earth was going on?

All of a sudden, the main motorway was upon her and she hadn't even noticed, quickly steering the car onto the slip road she joined the carriageway. Hers was the only car on the road, as usual, a lone crusader on the path to the daily grind. There would be the occasional lorry and maybe a tractor, but other than that she would be alone. She was not even in the mood to turn on the radio to listen to music this morning, normally something she loved and turned up loud, but not today.

Travelling the motorway on autopilot she failed to notice anything much at all. She had travelled this road every day for seven years, even when pregnant and throwing up in a carrier bag every ten minutes, always noticing the trees, the fields and the distant horizon where you could just make out the sea if you looked hard enough. But today it was a grey road with a destination that there was a duty to reach in order to carry out a job that had to be done.

Suddenly, out of thin air, with no warning, and like the majestic Pegasus bounding into view from a heavenly place, an enormous, beautiful stag was directly in front of her car. She saw beauty and could not erase it from this earth, so with lightning reflexes she jerked the steering wheel hard left.

Chapter 2
March – Love

Everything was black. Not just black but a dark inky black that felt claustrophobic and bottomless. Silence. She could see nothing and hear nothing. It was eerie, lonely and yet welcoming at the same time.

Squinting and concentrating really hard she could just make out a pinprick of light. Blinking and re-focusing the light seemed like it was coming towards her, gradually taking on size and substance. It felt warm on her face, comforting like the softest blanket, and soothing like her mother's embrace. All of her fears and negative thinking left her and disappeared into the black backdrop, she felt loved, wanted, at peace.

As the light drew closer, she could just make out the silhouette of a person. Recognition sparked in her but could not be placed immediately. Closer, warmer, more beautiful and more familiar.

'Grandad,' she said. 'Is that you?'

'It certainly is our Mand, what sort of mess have you created for yourself?'

'What do you mean, I don't know where I am?'

'You are here, and so am I. So, how shall we spend our time?'

'But you are dead, does that mean I am dead?' she asked.

'That, our Mand, is entirely up to you.'

His voice was soothing and made her feel at ease with the world. There was no longer fear and negativity, it had been replaced with pure love.

'I still don't understand?'

Still confused, she immediately loved this place and had always loved this man, but could not fathom what was happening to her. Was she dead? Was she dreaming? What exactly had happened to her?

'It's no use trying to work this out, our kid; it is what it is, and you are where you are. Now, what would you like to talk about?'

'I... I... I... don't, I don't know,' she managed to stutter.

'Now, that is not the girl I know; you always knew what to say and would never stop saying it.'

Mandy smiled; he knew her so well. He was her paternal grandad, George, or grandad whiskers as they had fondly called him as children due to his unusual beard. He was always jolly and loving with a Santa laugh and time with him had always been a blast. From playing in the sandpit he had made for them, to exploring his sheds which were like Aladdin's caves.

Deciding just to follow her gut she managed to speak.

'I have missed you so much.'

'I know you have, sweetheart, but what is more important is what are you going to do?'

'About what?'

'About this.'

She thought for a minute. Was he talking about where she was, or what had happened? Wait a minute. What HAD happened? She remembered being in the car and then the magnificent beast that had appeared out of nowhere.

'Did I kill the deer?'

'No, it was not his time,' he reassured her.

'Is it my time?'

'It is not like you to ask closed questions, so ask me something I might care to answer, we don't have much time.'

'Why am I here?' she managed to say.

'That is better. You are here because this morning that is what you wished for.'

'I didn't.'

'Oh, but you did. You could no longer see your purpose. You no longer saw what you had and how precious it is.'

She thought again. He was right, her thinking had been so negative and she had felt like there was no point in keeping going. *What had been the underlying reason for her thinking this way?* she wondered.

'But I do realise what I have. I love my children, please don't take me away from them. I will do anything to get back to them, anything,' she begged.

'Anything?'

'Yes, I said that!'

'Well then, maybe I can give you another chance to appreciate what you have.'

'You can do that?'

'No, not me, but I think I can influence the powers that be. Would you be up for a challenge?'

'Yes, anything!'

'Wait here, I will be right back.'

'No, don't leave me, I love having you here.'

The thought of him leaving her again suddenly filled her with grief and dread.

'I left a long time ago, but for now, I will be gone just a second.'

She sat alone again in the dark, yet she could see. She could see the faces of her children Becca and Dan. They were beautiful and she loved them so much. How could she have thought that her life was so meaningless, even for a second? Vowing to herself never to think like that again, no matter what was happening around her a cool breeze tickled her arm.

At that moment George returned.

'I have a challenge for you, it is agreed. You will return to your life, but you will not be perfect as you were, you experienced some physical trauma and your body needs to heal. You will experience a series of events, you will be given no information, no timescales and no help. You have to overcome these events in order to win your life back. Can you do this?'

'Of course, I will do anything!'

'I know you WILL do anything, but CAN you do this?'

'I CAN!'

He was gone, it was black.

'I am cold.'

She heard the sound of the sirens and saw the orange flashing lights.

Chapter 3
March – Realisation

'Can you hear me, love?'

'Yes,' Mandy said, 'I can hear you.'

She felt the paramedic trying to open the door of her car, it was jammed shut and needed some leverage. He checked her breathing, pulse and did a visual check to make sure that there were no bleeding injuries that required immediate attention. The car was wrecked. She could see the crumpled metal of the bonnet touching the windscreen and it was a tangled mess.

'Can you feel this, love?' he asked.

'Yes, I can, but it hurts.'

She winced with the shooting pain in her legs and up her back. She knew that this was not going to be good.

'You just stay still and let us move you onto this board, I am going to give you some pain meds, sharp scratch.'

She felt the needle pierce her skin and then floated onto the stretcher. The ambulance journey was like a weird roller coaster ride and her thoughts were out of her control. She could hear talking but it sounded a long way away. Soon enough, feeling a lot more lucid she was being moved onto a hospital bed.

'We are taking you for an X-ray, love,' the doctor said, 'we need to make sure that nothing is broken.'

'OK,' was all she could manage.

The X-ray machine was clumsy, and so was the nurse. Everything was hurting, the pain in her back and legs was like a drill, constant and annoying.

'I wonder what I have done?' she said to herself.

Then all of a sudden, she remembered the visit from her grandad, the beautiful place and the deal that had been made.

This is it, she thought, *I have been given a second chance and I am back to my life. I need to change things and I need to make big, BIG changes.*

That thought stayed with her and she started to consider exactly what changes were needed in her life. Her children were perfect, the dogs were also like her children, she loved them dearly and their care was never a problem to her. John, her husband, came into her head and the feeling was strangely indifferent. Why was that then?

Back on the ward, there were bandages all over her, a cast on her leg and a drip in her arm. Her injuries were severe but not life-threatening, the recovery would take about four months and there would be a need for some physio, but that was achievable.

Just as she was lost in thought, her husband John turned up with the children, looking worried and drawn. Was it worry? He almost looked more harassed, like this was an inconvenience, or was she seeing things that weren't there?

'Who called you?' she said.

'The ambulance crew found my number in your phone and they rang me while they were bringing you here.'

Becca and Dan started to climb on the bed to hug her when John snapped at them and told them to get off. It was aggressive, impatient and totally unnecessary. Glaring at him, a question came to her. Why was she with him? That thought had never occurred to her before. But at that moment when he had snapped so quickly and nastily at her beloved children, it occurred to her now.

Was this her first challenge? Was she going to look at everyone and everything and wonder that same thing? It started to dawn on her that the challenges ahead may well be more difficult than she had initially thought.

Looking again at the man she had spent all of those years with there was anger in his face. It wasn't just anger; it was something more. For now, she decided to ignore it but made a mental note.

Chapter 4
March – Thought

As the days passed, more practical tasks set in. Mandy had spoken to her employers, and they had been hugely supportive and told her to concentrate on getting well.

Her mum had visited and it had been so nice to see her, but she couldn't bring herself to tell anybody about what had happened because she feared that they would think that she had lost her mind. Not even her mum, who she had always discussed everything with.

Had she lost her mind? Did she imagine what had happened, was it just a dream or was it real? The feeling of warmth and love seeped over her and she knew that it was true, because if there had been anybody, she would have chosen to meet her, it would have been Grandad Whiskers. Replaying every second of the event in her mind, she held onto the memory and yearned to see him again, even just for a second. To touch him, to talk to him. Had she wasted the time they had?

Her sister Angel broke her thoughts when she arrived in her usual loud and animated style. She looked a bit distracted and not her usual self, but Mandy put that down to concern. Angel was her "little" sister and she had spent her life trying to follow in her big sister's footsteps but had failed. Mandy had helped Angel to achieve her dream of running a pub by buying her the lease at the Farmer's Arms and acting as a silent partner, pretty much letting her get on with it. Maybe there were some issues with the business, she made a note to pop in and support her sister when it was physically possible for her to do so.

Becca and Dan came regularly with their dad and were a complete joy every time they came; she treasured this opportunity to remain a part of their lives and would never be anything other than grateful. They were perfect little beings and she was so proud. It suddenly occurred to her just how lucky she was to have them at all! This thinking time in the hospital was giving her the opportunity to take stock. Having almost lost her life once before with a ruptured ectopic pregnancy, the doctors had told her then that she had only a slim chance of falling pregnant as they had needed to remove one of her fallopian tubes, but she defied the odds and Becca arrived two years later. They were happy with the one child, but fast forward another four years and a happy accident happened and Dan was born in April five months before her fortieth birthday, what a gift.

Suddenly a terrible memory popped into her head. Arguments that had occurred between her and John when she fell pregnant with Dan. He did not want any more children and told her that she had to have an abortion, he was too old to be a dad again and just couldn't be bothered. Horrified, Mandy had refused even though both her husband and his mother had bullied her constantly throughout the pregnancy until the final scan. John could do no wrong in his mother's eyes, she would believe anything he said and side with him every time. Maybe this was at the bottom of how she had been feeling the day of the accident. Perhaps the rot had set in then? She sat and thought about this for a long time, and the longer she thought, the more incidents of bullying became clear.

She was not a person to be bullied. She was a strong woman with a high-powered job and balls of steel at work. So, why had she allowed this man to bully her, and not even noticed? She felt overwhelmed with sadness. Had the children been bullied while she was at work for so many hours? Had they noticed the way he was with her? Was THIS one of her challenges? These thoughts weighed heavily, she felt weak, like she had failed herself and her children by putting up with behaviour that she would never tolerate anywhere else in her life.

Way too much thinking time!

Mandy pulled herself around and decided that if she was going to be off work for a while, she should do something really positive with her time. Something that could keep her mind busy and stop it from wandering off and imagining things. Opening her laptop, she started searching for self-development.

After hours of searching, she had decided to sign up for a couple of online courses that would give her some additional qualifications. You can never educate yourself too much, this had been a strong belief during her entire life. After achieving her A-Levels, she had gone on to university to study art and been successful. But due to a turn of events involving her sister (again!), with her mum and dad losing a lot of money on a hair salon they had bought for her; Mandy had needed to just get a job and help out.

Having worked for a wine merchant in the holidays and in a bar three evenings a week whilst at uni, she was familiar with the off-licence trade and had landed a job as a Wines and Spirits Supervisor in a largescale supermarket chain. This had been the beginning of her career and the art was parked for the sake of earning money. Her employer had supported her ongoing education and she had completed a Diploma in Management Studies and a Diploma in Leadership Coaching whilst working and was very proud of her achievements.

Perhaps this was one of her challenges, making the most of the downtime she had while she was off work, educating herself and gaining new skills. Well if it was, she was going to do it with knobs on! She signed up for two advanced Diploma's in NLP and Life Coaching and a Diploma in Building Self Confidence. Having touched on NLP during her management studies and been intrigued, she saw herself as a coach and a people person, so these courses made sense. She would go back to work in four months' time as an even better manager, challenge accepted.

Whilst signing up for the courses, she noticed something in the search results called "The Secret". It caught her eye and she checked it out. It sounded totally Americanised but something struck a chord, she had no idea what, but it was available on DVD so she ordered it and just thought she would watch it at some point when she was back at home.

Home, now that was a welcome thought.

Chapter 5
April – Home

Ten days had passed and it was finally time for her to go home. The doctors had said this was the day and she was really excited to see Becca, Dan and the dogs. Excited to hold them, smell them and just rejoice in the fact that they were hers, she had been given this second chance to be with them and was going to cherish every second.

Not so much John. Just going through the motions with him, being nice and saying she loved him and was pleased to be going home to him, but not feeling it. It was strange indeed, this was the man that she had once considered her soul mate; they had been close once, and he had been nice. What had happened?

Her thoughts were broken by the ringing of her mobile phone.

'Hi, Dad.'

'Hi, love, how are you doing?'

Just the sound of this man's voice made her feel warm and loved, the same feeling she had had when her grandad had been there with her in the blackness. She worshipped this man and it wasn't that long ago he had come to stay with them for a few days, in fact, it had been February and it was just coming up to mid-March now. Both him and his wife had been to visit. She cringed, his wife (the witch, aka Amy) really did not like her and her sister, but she was so close to her dad, that Amy had to put up with it. However, it was so easy to see in Amy's eyes that she resented her husband's love for his daughters, especially Mandy, his firstborn. There was a bond that she could not break, no matter how black her heart was or devious she was in her ways. Angel was another matter altogether, her lifelong problems with money management, debt and mental illness had made her an easy target for the new wife and currently, Angel and her dad were not speaking, a situation that had been manipulated by constant negative comments from Amy.

The witch could never come between Mandy and her dad though, although she made a mental note to try and repair his relationship with her sister Angel. Another challenge.

'I'm fine, Dad, a bit battered and bruised with some broken bits but I will survive. How are you?'

When he had visited in February, they had taken a really long walk and had one of those treasured once in a lifetime, long and honest talks that had felt so natural and beautiful. Mandy had felt so close to her dad but she also felt that he wasn't entirely happy with the witch or that there was something wrong. He had struggled when they had discussed his wife, looked sad when they had discussed Angel and looked in pain with his back. But he never complained, so she had let it go.

'Oh, I am OK, love, just getting old and creaky that's all. I will come up and see you as soon as you are settled back at home.'

'That would be lovely, I love you.'

'I love you too, speak soon.'

Just then the door opened and two very bouncy, excited little humans ran in, hugged and kissed her. At last, she was going home.

An hour later and she was walking through her front door to two hairy, bouncy excited family members who were also kissing her. This was it, there were four children, two of them fur babies, who loved her unconditionally and this is where her energy should be focused.

As soon as she was settled in and the kids and dogs had calmed down, she was able to set up her study space and get organised with what would become her life for the next few months while the children were at school. She had no money worries as her contract gave her twelve months' sick pay, so it was her duty to be doing something productive that would enhance her job when she returned to work. But first she had a DVD to watch. John was playing his stupid computer war games and the kids were happily playing so she turned on the DVD player.

Chapter 6
April – Revelations

She was blown away. Totally blown away. What had she just watched?

"The Secret" was not what she had expected, it was way more. Her neurons and synapses were firing on overload. This was possibly the most evoking and inspiring thing that she had ever watched in her life. Perhaps, this was one of her challenges, to really try and live the principles of the secret. It was amazing, it was Americanised, but it was amazing. She was determined to research all of the mentors, professionals and academics that appeared in it. Chicken soup for the soul here we come!

She was accumulating quite a list of things that could possibly be challenges, so she thought she should probably write them down so that she didn't forget anything.

She thought hard, there was her recovery; her marriage; her dad's relationship with her sister; check all was OK in the pub business; spending more time with the kids; studying; the secret. Quite a list already.

Any or none of the items on the list could be a challenge, she didn't know and so she was playing the safe game. The psychological aspect of not knowing what was coming and guessing if it was one of the set challenges was taking its toll. It was all-consuming in some ways and a release in others. She found herself looking around and wondering what was next, bracing herself, and in fight or flight mode. Mandy steadied herself and thought that she would need a robust coping strategy to enable her to have the strength to face what was to come. Filling her time productively with new skills, spending time with the kids making memories and dealing with things head-on was her strategy and she was going to stick with it.

She quickly settled back into a routine of getting up early, hobbling out with the dogs on crutches, good job they lived in the middle of nowhere, getting the kids ready and waving them goodbye while John took them to school. She had the full day after that to study, research and make plans to improve her life. Her injuries were improving daily and the pain was under control with drugs. She was moving more, feeling more energised and allowing her body to heal in its own time.

It was at this point that she noticed how little John actually did around the place. He would come home from the school run and do the bare minimum. She had to ask him to do things and each request would be met with a grumble because all he really wanted to do was play on his computer games.

She started to think back and realised that she had still done the lion's share of chores even when she had been working a sixty-hour week. The daily routine would consist of emptying the dishwasher, loading the washing machine, running the hoover round, walking dogs, going to work, coming home, unloading the dishwasher, cooking dinner, bathing the kids, reading to the kids, emptying the washer, loading the dryer, doing the ironing and going to bed exhausted. All of this while John was playing computer war games.

Resentment started to set in. Why had she let this become her life? Was it for an easy life? What was she thinking? She couldn't even answer her own questions. However, the one thing she did understand is that acting in anger allows no progress.

Confused, but convinced it was her fault for allowing it to get this bad, she decided to deal with it so that both adults in the house were taking equal responsibility. This would prove a more difficult task than she would have thought, but for now, it was a plan.

Studying and time with the kids were the highlights in Mandy's life and if these were challenges, they were a breeze. She had always had a level of inquisitiveness that had made learning new things easy, so the courses that were nine months in duration were taking weeks because of the amount of time available to study and by the end of April she had completed her first advanced diploma with a distinction.

April also saw a brief visit from her beloved dad, Brian, and she engineered her sister, Angel, to be in the same location as him and they actually spoke and got along like there had been no issues or timelapse. It made Mandy feel good to see two people she loved so much re-connected, she could tell how much they had missed each other and loved each other.

When it was time for him to return home to Manchester, those three hundred miles seemed an awful long way. There was an ominous feeling in the air and she hugged her dad just a little bit tighter as he got into the car to leave her, he really was a great man, she made a promise to go and see him more often.

When she thought about how she was doing with her potential challenges she was feeling quite smug.

'Bring it on!' she shouted out loud, 'I can deal with anything!'

Chapter 7
May – Spectrum

'Hello, is that Mrs King?'

'Yes, it is, how can I help you?' Mandy replied.

'This is Mrs Dunston, Daniel's head teacher, there has been an incident at school today that is quite concerning, would it be possible for you to come in for a meeting?'

Fortunately, Mandy had just been approved to drive again, although still a long way from recovery, she was able to do short journeys. She shouted at John and explained the scenario but he was in the middle of a game and didn't want to go, so off she went alone, wondering what Dan could have done that was so bad.

Assuring herself that it would be something and nothing, just "boy's stuff", she arrived at the school gates. As she entered Mrs Dunston's office, a feeling of unease crept over her, one that she had experienced a lot since the car accident. Being on the edge all of the time, not knowing if there was going to be a challenge, not certain about anybody's behaviour or any event, it was starting to make her feel things that were unusual and unexpected. However, she then surmised that this itself could be a challenge and would instantly put concerns out of her mind in case she failed. It was quite stressful actually, but it was better than being dead.

'Thank you for coming in so quickly, Mrs King, I think it is important to strike while the iron is hot.'

'I agree, so what has Daniel done that has prompted you to call me into school? I think this is the first time that I have been called in for either of them.'

'It certainly is, but Daniel has been demonstrating some quite violent and aggressive behaviour in the playground, that seems to be way beyond his years and when we try and deal with the behaviour he is reacting equally as violently.'

Mandy was stunned. Her sweet-natured little boy was showing violent behaviour, what on earth could have happened? Again, the feeling in her gut was physical, something was really wrong.

'I don't know what to say, other than I have had an accident and have been in hospital and that maybe it could have unnerved him?'

'We think it is more than that, Mrs King, in fact, I have taken the decision to contact the early intervention team to complete an assessment on him in school.'

Again, stunned. How can this have happened? If this was a challenge it was cruel to be using a four-year-old boy.

'Did you hear me, Mrs King?'

'Sorry, my mind must have wandered there, what is or who are the early intervention team?'

'They are a team of professionals working within the SEN system who assess young children in their learning environment.'

'Excuse my ignorance, but what is SEN.'

'Special Educational Needs.'

The ground may well have opened. Mandy was paralysed with shock, fear, concern and horror. Not because this was the worst thing that could happen to anybody, but because she had not seen a single thing wrong with Dan. She had given birth to him, breastfed him for two years, been there every single day of his life and they were bringing a stranger in to see if he had special needs.

'I am stunned; I have never even noticed that anything could be wrong.'

'Don't worry too much, see it as a helping hand and if there is something then it is better to catch it at a young age so that he can get the help he needs.'

The drive home was sombre. How was John going to react to this? Was this about how he treated her? She arrived home and sat in the car for about twenty minutes. When she finally found the courage to go in and tell John, his reaction shocked even her.

'There is nothing wrong with my fucking son, and no middle-aged busy body is coming into my home telling me that there is!'

'Do you not think that it is better to make sure?'

'No, I fucking don't; now, I don't want to hear another word about it, do you hear me?'

Again, stunned. She felt bullied and not heard, like her son's best interests were being ignored. Eventually, she decided to let John cool down and bring it up again in a day or so. Just as she made that decision, she heard him talking on the phone, obviously to his mother, and they were going at it hammer and tongue about how it was ridiculous and there was nothing wrong with his fucking son. Mandy just retreated back to her studies and thought that this might be a tough challenge and readied herself for the coming arguments.

That night when the children came in from school, she took them for a long walk with the dogs, made their favourite tea and let them make homemade pancakes for pudding. Apparently, it was the best day ever.

John played Call of Duty.

Chapter 8
June – Turmoil

As expected, there had been heated arguments with John about what was or what wasn't wrong with "his" son. This would be the same son that he never did anything with or took anywhere, and the one he tried to abort. Who was this man? She just didn't recognise him anymore. He was so angry, lazy and unmotivated. Everything was somebody else's fault and he was literally angry with everything and everyone.

Getting through to John on any level had become a daily challenge. He would have moments that he was nice and loving, but they were rare. He became more demanding of material things and seemed to "need" something on a daily basis.

By the time June came, John had joined a metal detecting club, coerced a metal detector out of Mandy and was out two nights a week at the club or detecting.

This was a huge relief for Mandy as it meant she had quality time with the kids and could do things with them. They did the three-park challenge where they visited three parks in one evening then picked up the dogs and went to the beach with a picnic. The pleasure in this time with her children was without measure and if it was a challenge, it really didn't matter because it was the greatest time of her life.

The school made contact to say that the early intervention team had assessed Dan in school and they would like to come out and see Mum and Dad. John refused, so an appointment was set up with Mandy.

When the day came, it was nerve-racking, but also a relief. The lady who came was lovely, really lovely. She outlined her findings and it turned out that during the times that Mandy had been at work and in hospital, John had been allowing his four-year-old son to play on PEGI 18 war games, which would not normally have had such a huge impact if they did not think he was on the spectrum, but she definitely thought that he was.

'Whoa, slow down, what spectrum?' Mandy asked.

'Sorry, Mrs King, I was getting ahead of myself, I do think that Daniel is on the Autism Spectrum. I am not sure where he will be placed, he could have Dyspraxia; Asperger's or be autistic, he will need to be properly assessed.'

Mandy had heard of all of these disorders but really knew nothing about them. When you don't understand them then fear could set in.

'Please explain more about each of these things, I just don't know anything and that makes it difficult for me to understand what you are saying about options.'

A long conversation followed, which was both informative, less scary and the start of a journey. In Mandy's opinion, this could well be the first really big challenge that she had to face, so she was going to do it with her eyes wide open.

If her son was autistic, then she would find out everything about it and learn how to be the parent he needed, she had her doubts about John doing the same.

John was too late home that night to be able to discuss what had been said at the visit. Mandy was up early with the kids and dogs and was just making packed lunches when John's phone pinged in the utility room. He was still in bed, so she went through to see if it was urgent and saw that it was a message from another woman. Not knowing if she should look, she put it down and went back to lunches.

But it was niggling, so she went back and had a look.

'Last night was amazing; I can't wait until Thursday. Xx.'

Relief. Not anger, nor jealousy, just relief. Someone who has no clue how to end a marriage and be the "bad one" who broke up the home, had just been given the biggest gift ever. She would play the long game with this one and let him show his hand. This would fall right into her lap, although there was fear about being a single parent, there was more fear for her and the kids in staying in an environment of neglect, bullying and inequality.

After the school run Mandy set off for her arranged visit to her sister at the pub, hoping that all would be good and that if there were any problems that she could get them sorted out for her. On the way to the meeting, there was a call from her employer asking if she could go in for a meeting with the new manager tomorrow. She didn't even know that there was a new manager, she felt completely out of touch and resolved to rectify that when she went in for the meeting.

Nothing that she couldn't handle.

Chapter 9
June – Debt

The pub looked amazing, really clean downstairs and ready for business. However, upstairs Mandy was met with a completely different picture.

'What happened here, Angel?'

'Nothing, I knew you would come in and criticise; we can't all hit your high standards you know!'

'Slow down, I only asked what had happened.'

Angel burst into tears, hysterical tears, and managed to intermittently blurt out that she was not coping with running the pub, it was harder than she had imagined and that YOU have no idea how hard it is. She was a mess, obviously out of control and obviously struggling.

This was Angel though, she seemed to have a very short attention span. She would go into something all guns blazing and it would be the best idea ever, and within weeks or maybe months if you were lucky, it was the worst thing she had ever done.

Infuriated Mandy replied, 'Well, this is what you wanted, you all but begged me to do this for you and you told me that you would work any hours to make it work.'

'Well, I didn't think it would be so hard. And here I am again, the failure who can't cope, the one who is crap at everything and the one that makes a mess of everything.'

This was Angel's long-established tactic to lessen the blow, make everyone feel sorry for the younger sibling who had followed her more intelligent and prettier sister through life being "the black sheep" as she put it. Manipulative but actually it had worked on Mandy, her mum and her dad for years. They all just gave in, bailed her out, paid the debt and went without. In fact, over the years the bailouts from Mandy alone totalled tens of thousands. It felt very much like Groundhog Day, so Mandy steadied herself and decided to be calm.

'Well, let's talk about exactly how hard this has been for you and how I can help you to sort it out. You know I will support you, it is in my best interest to do so, and you are my sister and I love you so, where shall we start?'

Angel looked up with that winning smile and said, well the stock take wasn't good and I am behind with the bills.

'OK, then let's start there then.'

For the next few hours, while the kids were at school, Mandy went through the last six stock take figures and asked for all of the invoices. She was shocked when Angel opened a chest of drawers and it was full to the brim with unpaid bills. This was going to take more than one day and it was obvious that there was a LOT of stock missing, mainly beer, mainly the beer that Angel's husband drank. The fact that Gareth was an alcoholic, which had been discussed at the time and Angel had sworn on her life that it would not be an issue, was hitting Mandy in the face with a big fat "I told you so". She had her doubts at the time, but her heart had ruled her head because Angel was a disaster, she had constantly failed, and to a certain and very irrational extent Mandy felt wholly responsible. Crazy and unreasonable, but that is families for you.

So, because she "had it all" and Angel had nothing, Mandy had bought the lease and given her the free reign in the pub. She knew she should have checked up on her and that Angel was not good at anything with responsibility, but she really wanted to believe that her sister could do this, so she threw caution to the wind and dived in.

Mandy made arrangements in her diary to come back the day after tomorrow; let's face it, there was nothing planned other than study and play with the kids, and this was urgent.

Having the same gut feeling that she had at the school only a week or so ago, she was wondering if this was her next challenge. She needed her best business head on for this one, so she decided to have an early night, not bother talking to John and just get her meeting at work out of the way tomorrow. The doctors had said she could go back to work in a few weeks so at least she had some good news for them.

Chapter 10
June – Surprise

Mandy arrived at her workplace early as was the norm and headed in to see the team. They were so pleased to see her; they had missed her and the place wasn't the same without her. When was she coming back? How was she feeling? She looked so well; they had been worried. All of the usual responses.

They were an amazing team and she truly loved them and had missed them, so she was keen to meet with the new manager and sort out a return-to-work date.

Sitting at her desk and going through her e-mails, it felt like familiar territory. That gut feeling was back though, she wondered why because this was merely a formality.

When she was asked to come in by her friend in HR, she had no idea who she was meeting. Entering the room, she was met by a stern-looking woman, who was most unpleasant.

'Sit.'

'Nice to meet you, I am Mandy and I would like to thank you for arranging this return-to-work meeting today.'

'Who told you this was a return-to-work meeting?' the new manager asked.

'Well, nobody, I just assumed.'

'Never assume. I would like to start the meeting by offering you the right to representation.'

'Hold on a minute, is this a disciplinary meeting?' Mandy inquired.

'No, but you are entitled to representation,' was the stern woman's response.

'No, I'm fine.'

'Right, then I will proceed. You have been off work now for a couple of months. It is very difficult from a moral perspective and a cost perspective to keep senior managers on paid sick leave. We as a company can't even recoup these costs as you allege to have almost collided with a deer and swerved to miss it, therefore there is no third party to pay compensation.'

The stern woman looked very serious.

Mandy looked stunned. Are they saying this is my fault because I didn't hit the deer? Are they saying I am lying? Questions and confusion raced through her head. What was going on? She totally understood the need to manage absence and the impact it had on the bottom line. She also understood that she was key to the business performance, but surely, they should have put a replacement manager in during her recovery and she could not be blamed for what happened while she wasn't there.

'Whilst you have been away the sales have not been as good and profits are down. When this is an issue, we have to cut costs, the biggest cost savings are when we trim management, not staff. We would like to offer you a severance package to leave the company today.'

This woman didn't understand the business; the sales were down because the team had no leader and had lost motivation. Instead of cutting costs they should have invested in people.

'Today?'

'That is correct, we would like to offer you three months' salary to leave today.'

That was the offer on the table.

'I need to think about this.'

'That is fine, why don't you go and get yourself a coffee and think about our offer?'

Mandy went to the coffee shop, stopping every ten seconds to speak to another member of staff. She sat and drank her coffee in a remote corner.

This is a big challenge, she thought, and *how I respond to it could be life-changing.* She reviewed where she was. She had completed two of her study courses; she had researched and developed a plan for how she was going to make change; her husband was having an affair and she faced being a single mum; Dan was in the system being diagnosed for autism and would need her; Angel was in trouble. The decision she made today would set her on a path for a complete change. This surely was a big challenge and would require courage.

She made her way back to the office and sat down.

'I will go today, no questions asked, no challenges now or in the future for constructive dismissal or discrimination, if you give me twelve months' salary.'

The area manager looked at her, red in the face and said, 'Nine months.'

'No, twelve months or I take you to a tribunal for everything and anything and you and I both know that will cost you more in time and money than paying me what I ask and you still might have to pay me, so the way I see it, you should cut your losses.'

'You will leave now?' the stern woman asked now almost puce in colour.

'Like a silent mouse and I will say nothing.'

So that was that. Challenge met head-on and deal done, she was unemployed but quite wealthy. Certainly, wealthy enough to start her own business and sort out the pub.

Mandy felt smug, yet again. Some serious challenges had been laid before her and she felt like she was making the right decisions. She was still here so she must be doing OK.

Tomorrow she would sort out the pub and help her sister.

Chapter 11
June – Ultimatum

Being so decisive felt empowering. All of the principles in "The Secret" were about positive thought, visualisation, making clearly defined decisions and Mandy had been working hard on her positivity and visualisation. This wasn't too much of a task as she had always been a "glass half full" type of person and her career had readied her for change; in fact, she thrived on it.

But this was also scary shit. She had never been out of a highly paid job since her early twenties and she was now forty-four and jobless. As she drove home that day, she didn't even care what John thought or how he would react. She was going home to tell him that she had been the main earner for long enough and that it was time for him to get a full-time job while she thought about what she had wanted to do, no arguments. If that didn't push him towards the other woman then she would be surprised.

When she arrived home, he was there drinking coffee still unshaven and in his pyjamas. Entering with a purpose he was told what had happened and for the second time today she watched someone go red in the face and say their words through gritted teeth.

'You have done what?' he managed to spit out.

'I have made the decision to take a severance package and think about what I want to do, you need to get a full-time job as soon as possible and take some responsibility for a change,' Mandy replied assertively.

This did not go down well. John did not like to work. Mandy had met him following several years on her own after the very bitter breakdown of her second marriage. She had married two bad boys and both had ended in disaster. She often said that she was better at picking staff than picking husbands and her team at work thought this was hilarious. Here, she was facing the possibility of a third failed marriage, but John was not a bad boy like the others, she actually married him because he was the nice guy. He was the opposite of the first two and having failed twice, Mandy had decided that if she were to ever marry again, she would choose with her head.

She had actually stayed on her own for about five years after her second marriage broke down and concentrated on her career, which had paid dividends in promotions, salary increases, company cars and the like.

So, when she met John on a chance visit home to her mum's he was so nice, so different and so complimentary. This was what she needed after so many years alone. All was good with them until her ectopic pregnancy. They had not been trying for a baby and Mandy had almost died, so it had a profound effect on them in that they both wanted to have a child, which had not been on the cards before.

When they fell pregnant, against the odds they were delighted and thought that this would be the icing on the cake for their relationship. They were both overjoyed when Becca arrived prematurely at a mere five pounds, she was their world. Unfortunately, Becca was very ill as a baby and spent her first Christmas in the hospital due to a febrile fit and subsequently diagnosed renal reflux and kidney problems. After that she was more important than John, so he was a little pushed out, however, they trundled along. When the pregnancy with Dan happened and the terrible bullying started, things were not good and they had been cruising since.

Not wanting to break up the family, Mandy realised that she had been making do and just going with the flow while John did what he wanted with her money. She could see how he would resent being told to get a job now, but she was not going to budge.

John said he would try and that he was going out and Mandy said that suited her just fine. She sat with her studies and thought about what she would do. Maybe she could start a coaching business with her new qualifications, that was a thought.

Above all else, she was keen to stay on top of her challenges. She really felt like she was doing OK and handling everything that was being thrown at her quite well, although she was a bit uneasy at the rate things had been thrown at her this month and hoped that whoever the challenger was, they were going to slow it down a bit going forward.

Chapter 12
June – Plan

There is no time like the present, especially when you are playing with your life pitched against a set of challenges.

Back at the pub with Angel, Mandy continued to go through the stock takes and the invoices. She paid the urgent ones, helped to clean up, had a meeting with the whole team, set some goals and got everyone motivated to really go for it.

Angel felt much better and was really positive about all the things they had discussed regarding turning the business around. They had a plan; they had some buy-in and things seemed a little more positive than two days ago.

Despite all of this, that gut feeling was back. Mandy couldn't put her finger on it. Gareth had point-blank denied drinking the beer or giving it away so Mandy had arranged for the brewery to come in and do a complete stock take and audit in two weeks' time on the fourteenth of July.

There was nothing more she could do here and needed to give them a bit of space to get on with turning things around.

She went home to talk to John about Dan. This was going to be interesting.

'I know that he is your son and you love him, but he is struggling and we need to accept help for him so that he can cope, this is not about your stupid pride,' was where they were at in the conversation.

'But I don't think there is anything wrong with him,' John replied.

'I know, neither do I, he is perfect to me, but I don't want him getting into trouble or being picked on because we didn't listen or get him help. They were concerned about him playing adult rated games, have you been allowing him to do that?' she asked him.

'Yes, I didn't think it would do any harm.'

'That is their point, it may not have done any harm if he wasn't autistic, but he is struggling with separating fiction and reality and right and wrong. We have to show him the way and I am telling you now, he does not play on those games again, it is Sonic the Hedgehog only. OK?'

'Whatever you say, I am going out detecting.'

'Where are you going tonight, then?'

'Oh, just to a field in Coldstream.'

'Have fun,' she said with more than a hint of sarcasm.

Mandy knew he was lying and that the whole metal detecting ruse had been so that he could see the other woman, but she would bide her time and wait, she knew how to wait.

Mandy packed the dogs in the car, set off for the school run and felt like she was in control. They would do the three-park challenge again and then get fish and chips at Seahouses while the dogs had a run on the beach. Life was good and she felt like she was winning.

Chapter 13
July – Cancer

Things had settled down a bit after the run of challenges in June. Dan had been for two assessments and they were told that it would take time, since it was such a big spectrum and that it could sometimes be difficult to get a diagnosis quickly. He was no longer playing on the games; the early intervention team were working with the school to deal with some of his issues and he was feeling better.

Angel seemed to be coping better, Mandy had popped in for a coffee and a chat a couple of times being big sister and trying to be supportive, but Angel was good at hiding things so she was never totally convinced.

She had spent some quality time with her mum and the kids and talked about what may happen soon with John. Her mum admitted to never liking him nor thinking he was good enough. She understood as a mum that nobody would ever be good enough so did not take offence.

The gut feeling was back and there seemed to be no reason. It had been a fairly good indicator thus far about bad news, but all was quiet. Little did she know that her world was about to be rocked on its axis.

It was a Tuesday evening on the seventh of July and the phone rang. The ring seemed louder and more urgent than normal, but how could that be? Mandy answered the phone and on the other end was the witch. Her dad's wife Amy. This was odd as she never called.

'Hi, Amy, is everything OK?' Mandy asked her, genuinely concerned.

'No, it's not really, it's your dad, he has cancer.'

The world stopped.

NO, YOU CAN'T DO THIS!

This is not fair play; why would you do this to me? I love that man. He is your son!

Eventually, Mandy found the words to reply.

'How bad is it?'

She knew though, she knew. Her gut was going wild and she felt physically sick.

'It's terminal, they think he might have a year. They can't find the source, it's in his blood, but also in his lymph nodes as well. He is starting chemo tomorrow.' Amy managed to say whilst sobbing a little.

Mandy knew where the source was, even before the doctors. He had been having trouble with his back. When he was a teenager, he had stupidly dived into a pond without checking the depth and broken his neck. He had spent six months in hospital in a plaster and they had taken a bone out of his leg to put into his neck. He never had good movement in his neck and back, in fact, he had failed his driving test six times for not looking in the mirror properly, only passing on the seventh attempt after telling the instructor about his injury.

He had always looked like turning his head was hard work and the problems with his neck had led to problems with his back. She was sure this is where cancer had attached itself.

'I am coming down, Amy,' Mandy insisted.

'He doesn't want everyone coming down visiting, in fact, I have not told him it is cancer, he doesn't need to know. I have asked the doctors to only communicate with me about his condition and say nothing to him,' was the very defensive sounding response.

What did she say? Why on earth was she not allowing him to know what was wrong? What was going on with her?

'Well, I am coming down anyway, he is my dad and I love him so I will be there this week sometime, I will let you know when.' Mandy was insistent, nobody was keeping her from her beloved dad.

Mandy hung up and wanted to scream. Why would you take such a good man? How was she going to cope with this? What strategy could she adopt to stop her going down and to keep her forward-thinking? She picked up her diary, started to capture her feelings and then she picked up the phone to call Angel, knowing that this would be the second hardest call she would ever have to make.

'Angel, I have something to tell you that is very upsetting so can you make sure you are not in the pub.'

'Wait a minute, then I will go upstairs, I hope you are not going to have a go at me again,' she said, hackles already up. 'Right, I am upstairs, so what is wrong now?'

Mandy braced herself and tried to find the right words, but they just wouldn't come. Angel and dad had just reconciled, and now he would be taken away, she just hoped that her sister would be able to cope with the news.

'There is no easy way to tell you this. Dad has cancer, it's terminal. I am going down on Friday; do you want to come with me?'

Silence. Then sobbing. Her little sister was breaking her heart and this was breaking Mandy's too.

'Angel, I know how you feel honestly, but we need to be strong for him, and we need to see him.' Mandy tried hard to reassure her sister.

'I know, I can't process this right now, I need to go.'

And she hung up.

Mandy decided to give her time to cry, to be angry and then she would go over in the morning for coffee and a hug. They would make plans to go and see their dad and talk about how they would cope. This was surreal. Mandy took out the diary again and captured her thoughts. At that moment, it struck her that she should feel this fully and write it down. Maybe in doing that it would not only help herself but may actually help someone else in the future. The decision was made, she would track this journey, emotional as it would be and write a book.

Even John was struggling with this news, he was actually being very loving and supportive. The kids did not need to know yet, they really loved their grandad and although Becca may understand at nine, Dan would not at four.

Thinking about what had happened in the last few weeks, Mandy acknowledged that leaving her job had been the right decision, after all, now she could spend some quality time with her dad while she still had him.

While she still had him. She was going to lose him; it was out of her control. The woman he married would make all of the decisions and she would have no input. She had never felt so sad, so helpless and so damn angry before in her life. She wrote that down, closed the diary and cried herself to sleep.

Chapter 14
July – Visiting

Two days after that phone call Mandy and Angel were driving the three hundred miles to Manchester to see their dad. Mandy was trying to keep the conversation upbeat but she could see that her sister was struggling.

They had decided to go down, just the two of them to assess the situation, talk to Amy and the doctors and to get a grip on exactly what was happening and how long they had.

Mandy was writing in the diary on a regular basis. It really was an effective way of dealing with the pain. Even so, she was surprised at the amount of comfort she achieved from writing everything down. She wasn't concerned about grammar or the story, she wanted to keep it real and raw because that is what the cancer journey is like.

'Have you thought about how you are going to get through this?' Mandy asked Angel.

'I just can't think about it; I feel so bad for not speaking to him for the last couple of years. I can't even remember why now. You kept telling me to make the first move and I was stubborn and just wouldn't budge. I really wish I had listened to you.' Angel responded with obvious regret.

'You never listen to me, and you can't beat yourself up, it took both of you for it to go on for so long.' Again, Mandy was trying hard to reassure her sister and keep her from the black hole of depression that she regularly went down into.

'But I am beating myself up, I wasted all that time.'

Angel burst into tears.

'Look, it is what you do and what you say now that matters. He needs you to just be you, to love him and to make him feel safe. Pull yourself together and find it in you to face this without breaking down. He is the one in the worst situation.'

This time she was more assertive.

Mandy really didn't know where her words were coming from. She was being so stoic and practical. The writing seemed to be such a powerful tool in removing the confusion from her head.

Angel had pulled herself together and was feeling a little better again.

'I know you are right, but I am not as strong as you.'

'I think you underestimate yourself, treat him like one of the old people you used to care for and just care for him.'

Back to a calm reassuring tone, it was often like this with her sister after so many years of trying to help her.

'I will try.'

'Well, that is all you can do.'

The drive was long and the emotions were up and then down. They shared memories from when they were children of "big kissy time", where their lovely dad would pin them down and kiss their faces until they laughed themselves purple. Then there was "big lickey time" which was way worse with his cigar breath. When they lived in the pub as children, they would take turns in going down in the Dumb Waiter in the bar at night and dad would sneak them a coke and a packet of crisps each without mum knowing.

The holidays they had in Blackpool when he would always buy a "kiss me quick" hat and wear it every day, much to the embarrassment of mum, and they would eat hot meat pies, hot doughnuts and make songs up about them.

He had to go on every ride, he was just full of fun. Then there were the holidays abroad where he would be constantly fooling around in the sea or the pool and throwing them in. They both smiled and realised just how lucky they had been to have this man in their lives. He had made their childhood full of smiles.

When mum decided she didn't want to be married to him anymore, for whatever her reasons were, it broke him. He had actually turned to Angel then for support as Mandy was away working, and she had supported him. Mandy reminded her about this and said that she was sure he would always be grateful for having her at that time.

Unfortunately, in his desperation to not be alone, he had made a couple of bad choices in women. He desperately tried to find a replica of mum and in doing so failed to see the real person. When he eventually met Amy, she was already connected to the family, vaguely as a friend of an aunt, but she was poison. She had an opinion about everyone and judged harshly. The most unforgiving person Mandy had ever come across; she was always going to be a challenge. When they married however, she chipped away at her dad with every mistake both of his daughters had ever made. Never recognising good and just repeating mistake after mistake, until he saw both girls in a different light. Mandy not so much as most of her mistakes had been down to bad choices in men, but Angel was a moving target and Amy hit the bullseye.

Mandy knew though that the resentment must be put to the side when they were in Manchester because there was no point in making what time he had left difficult, so she would be nice. Right to the end, she would be nice, and then she would close that chapter and never see Amy again.

'How are you feeling about Amy?' Mandy asked her sister.

'I HATE her and I don't know if I can be nice to her' was Angel's harsh response, but she could totally understand it.

'I know that, but can you dig deep and follow my lead? Let me do the talking and just speak when you need to. OK?'

'I will try,' was Angel's subdued reply.

That would have to do then.

Ahead of them, they saw the sign "Christies NHS Foundation Trust" and they entered the car park. Mandy's gut was sending signs once again; the atmosphere was foreboding.

They parked the car and made their way to the ward. Amy was waiting at the door like a custodian. Mandy greeted her in a friendly manner and Amy showed them in.

There he was, looking like a little old man, he must have lost two stone since they saw him in April. Gone was the larger-than-life funny man, replaced with this shadow. Still, there was a big grin on his face and Mandy felt like her heart was being squeezed. They spent their hour and he was chipper and telling jokes. But in between the jokes he would tell them that there was a mafia family on the ward and he had to hide his valuables. He would get out his notepad and try and solve complex math problems.

Brian King had been an electrical engineer, working in the middle east for BP and Shell. He had a big job and earned a big wage, which kept the family in a lifestyle of abundance. His charisma was like a magnet, he was the boss, but everyone loved him. BK the Big Man, cigar-smoking, bling wearing, designer brands and wads of fifty-pound notes, no more. At some point in life, we are all reduced to what clothes we are buried in and this was never more prevalent than right now for the two girls who had adored that big man.

'Right, Dad, we are going to head off now,' Mandy said as the visiting bell rang.

He looked sad. Mandy's heart broke. She didn't want to leave.

'We will be back next week though,' she reassured him and felt like that was all she had done today, reassure everyone else. *What about my needs?* she thought.

He smiled. Mandy had made the decision that she would make this journey every week now for as long as he had, it was non-negotiable.

They left the hospital ward with Amy shuffling behind them. She asked if they would like to come to the house for a sandwich before they drove back. Mandy accepted gracefully and they followed her to the house.

An hour was as much as either of the girls could stomach. They had made polite conversation and eaten her really rather awful sandwiches. During the conversation, Amy had mentioned in passing that, "Your dad has asked to re-do his will," so she was going with the solicitor tomorrow. Mandy knew what this meant, that everything was going to Amy. She didn't care; she just wanted her dad, if that was important to Amy then she could have it all.

They headed home feeling like time was running out. The doctors had said that there was no point in chemo as the cancer had progressed too far. He would be lucky to have six months. Mandy thought that they were being generous, but hoped for six months.

They arrived home at around ten o'clock, after a sixteen-hour day. Mandy came in exhausted but took the time to update John, who said he wanted to go the following week. She then updated her diary making sure to capture every emotion from the day. Sleep then took her fierce and hard and all she saw in her dreams was her grandad and she wanted to scream, "WHY?" But she had nothing left, so sleep won the battle.

Chapter 15
July – Stock Take

It was the fourteenth of July, five days after their visit to Manchester and Mandy planned to go again tomorrow with John and Becca.

Today was the day that the brewery was coming in to do the stock take and audit. Angel was in meltdown again, not coping well with her dad or the problems at the pub. But this needed to be done if there was any chance of moving the business forward.

Mandy realised that whatever the outcome, she was going to have to be heavily involved in the solution as Angel would not be able to do this alone. As much as this is not what she wanted to do, Mandy had always taken her responsibilities very seriously and faced problems head-on. This was no different.

At this point in the game, almost four months since the accident, Mandy was no longer wondering what was a challenge and what was not, there was just too much going on. Dan was still being assessed, her marriage was still rocky, her dad was dying, the pub was a huge risk, she was still recovering from her injuries and she had lost her substantial income. On the plus side, she had completed all three qualifications; had started writing a book and was considering signing up for a psychology degree with the Open University because she had enjoyed the diplomas so much. She was managing to spin all of the plates and still develop herself. It was not easy, but she knew what was at stake here and she was not leaving her children under any circumstances.

The stock take team arrived and looked very serious. The area manager pulled her to the side and expressed his concerns over the stock. Mandy agreed and said she would do her best to get things sorted out.

Rather than get in their way, she went home, gave them her number and instructed them to call her if they needed anything. She knew it would be the beginning of next week before they had a result and a report, so it was not worth worrying about. It would be whatever it was and she would take it from there.

Angel was still so volatile and upset that she wasn't going to visit her dad tomorrow, but she had planned to go early next week when the pub was quiet with Gareth and both her sons Nathan and Jack but she was leaving her daughter Emma with Mum because she was too little at three. That meant that they were managing two visits a week between them. Mandy had to pay for the fuel as she had no money, but that was nothing new.

This juggling of major events had become the new reality for Mandy. Her twenty-five years as a senior manager had prepared her for this. In her job she had juggled, solved and found new problems daily, that was the job. The difference was that none of the work problems was personal. None could hurt her or her children and her life never depended on them, so this was a whole different ball game.

She was ready to spend some time with her kids and have an early night.

Chapter 16
July – Visit Two

Dan was staying with Nana, which meant he was going to be spoiled all day.

Mandy, John and Becca left at nine o'clock so that they could make the 2 p.m. visiting time.

It was a much more upbeat car journey than the previous week. Mandy and John kept the mood light for Becca's sake, she was so excited about going to see her grandad.

They managed the journey in three hours, so they went for something to eat before visiting. Mandy had spoken to Amy and asked her to give them this time alone with her dad, she had agreed reluctantly, she was keeping his demise tightly under her wing and did not want to relinquish control.

When they arrived on the ward Becca bounced in and landed on her grandad giving him the biggest kiss and cuddle of his life. There was a tear in his eye and a break in Mandy's heart. There would be so few opportunities to see that happy picture again; in fact, she had the feeling that time was really running out, her dad looked like death, and her gut was going again.

They talked and John was absolutely amazing, cracking jokes with his father-in-law and taking the lead in the conversation. They all humoured him when he told them about the mafia in the hospital, and John left Mandy and her dad alone for fifteen minutes before the visiting ended taking Becca for a treat.

As she left Becca jumped on her grandad again and sweetly and innocently said, 'Grandad, I love you to the moon and back, and every night I say, I see the moon and the moon sees me, God bless, Grandad and God bless me.'

He was amused, touched and felt ten feet tall. Her love was so pure, so innocent and so true. Those would be the last words she would ever speak to him.

When they were finally alone, Mandy and her dad held hands.

'I've had a good run love,' he said.

At only sixty-seven he really hadn't and she was not ready to let him go.

'You have plenty of time yet, Dad.'

'I don't think so. I am tired. I loved seeing Becca today, but please don't bring her again, I don't want her to remember a dying old man,' he pleaded.

Amy may have kept his condition from him, but he was no fool. When it is your time, we all know.

'I won't, Dad, I just wanted her to see you again.'

'I know, and she has made me feel happy and loved today. Don't be afraid, it is OK, I am ready to see my dad again, I know he is there, and I know you know.'

Again, she was stunned at this statement. Was he rambling or did he actually know?

Was it his time or was this a challenge? A mist of confusion came over her once again. Why would you take your own son in order to test someone's strength, but then she stopped and thought, *But that is not the first time that has happened is it?* She had not been a person of faith for so many years, but at that moment all seemed clear, just for a moment.

'Look, Dad, let's just enjoy our time. I will come every week, whether you like it or not. I don't care what you look like and it is not a problem for me. Now, I have a long journey and a tired little girl. Our time for today is almost up. I love you to the moon and back.'

'And I love you, you have been my joy since the day you were born. I am proud of who you are.'

Mandy had to say goodbye quickly at that moment, so she kissed him and turned her back, and as soon as she did the tears flowed freely and didn't stop until she saw her daughter and composed herself. Heartbroken yet again. This was hard.

Chapter 17
July – Practicalities

The next day Mandy got back to some sort of normal life and planned some activities with the kids. She knew that she had only a few days before the reports were back for the stock take and audit so she may as well enjoy this time with her family.

John was like a different person all of a sudden. He was almost back to the nice guy she met and this was even more confusing as it was an emotionally charged time and things can look different when emotions are on alert. He had found a job, not a great job, but a job and that had taken the pressure off financially so that she didn't have to use all of her severance settlement. She could almost think she cared about him again and that there was light at the end of this particular tunnel. Perhaps forgiveness was one of her challenges? Still working on the principles of "The Secret", Mandy was finding it easier to just let things go and keep herself focused on her vision of the future.

Did it or did it not include John? She could not answer that yet.

The following Monday, the area manager from the brewery called and asked if they could make an appointment to meet on Wednesday the twenty-second of July. Angel was going to see their dad on Tuesday and Mandy was going on Friday so that fit well with the plans.

Mandy called her sister to tell her to make arrangements to be free on Wednesday and she agreed.

Wednesday arrived and Angel was still emotional from her visit to Manchester the previous day. Mandy could tell that her sister was on the edge and just hoped she could hold it together for the meeting.

The area manager, stock taker and auditor arrived and Mandy made them coffee and settled them in. There was no point in beating around the bush, so they commenced the meeting immediately.

The stock taker presented his findings, the auditor presented hers and the area manager summed up. Mandy sat motionless looking at Angel who was staring at her shoes and rocking back and forth.

Beers and ciders – £37,009

Wines and Spirits – £4,761

Cash losses – £1,276

Outstanding invoices – £22,893

Additional unpaid invoices found on-premises (some with court orders) – £14,112

Total – £80,051

She had managed in the space of ten months to lose this amount of money. Mandy had paid £12,000 for the lease so the debt was just under £100k.

The area manager said we could try and work out a payment plan. The Brewery team would help to create an action plan for the business. Mandy agreed and asked him if he could meet her at the pub on Thursday the thirtieth of July, that was the plan.

Everyone left and Mandy and her sister sat opposite each other in the office. Mandy was waiting for her to say something. Nothing, just shoe staring and rocking.

'Well, have you nothing at all to say?' Mandy asked eventually.

'No,' was the curt response.

'That is not good enough. You have been irresponsible with money in the past, but this is just beyond even my imagination. How the hell do you expect us to get out of this?'

'I don't fucking know!' Angel screamed.

She stood up, threw her chair across the room and just started screaming uncontrollably. Even Mandy was taken aback by this display and there was something seriously wrong with her sister. Was this an act to get out of the debt, or was she having a breakdown? Mandy was suspicious but also cautious.

'Well, I suggest you try and calm yourself down. I will arrange the staffing for the next few days. Nobody orders anything from anywhere without my sign off. I am taking the cheque books, the cash other than the till float and I will come and cash up each evening and remove the takings from the premises. Do you understand?'

'You don't fucking trust me, do you?' she screamed.

'No, I don't actually, so that settles that. You have just landed me in a whole lot of trouble at a time when I don't even have any income. You have nothing that you can say right now to make me even want to listen to you. I am going to call a solicitor to check my legal status, you just need to go somewhere quiet and think.'

At that, Mandy left the room and left her little sister crying. All that she could think of was, *Oh my fucking God!*

Chapter 18
July – Mountains

The visit to Manchester was a blur. Her dad looked no better but no worse. She had gone alone this time so that she could talk to him. Not wanting to burden him with her problems but also not wanting to lie, she had revealed what had happened.

'It's only money, love. I know it's a lot, I know your sister is ill and unable to manage money, but what I also know is that you will sort this out. I have complete faith in you,' he had said, and he was right.

That was such a comfort. Her mind had been all over the place since yesterday. She had argued with John for hours when she had arrived home and told him. The solicitor had confirmed that as a silent partner she was still one hundred per cent liable for all of the debt. John hated Angel anyway, but this was like lighting the blue touch paper. She had endured a constant bombardment of, "I told you so," and, "You should have listened to me." To be fair, he did tell her not to do it at the time because Angel could not be trusted, but that didn't feel any better when it was being rammed down your throat.

Driving to Manchester on her own had given her peaceful thinking time, and she felt like she had to have a plan before she met with the area manager next Thursday. This mountain looked pretty steep from where she was standing.

After talking to her dad for an hour, well, he fell asleep three times, so it was more like twenty minutes, she set off to head back home.

Deciding to be mindful and look for the beauty surrounding her on her route she started to calm down and formulate her plan.

Her dad was right; it was only money, she would trade every penny for his life, so her climbing boots were on and she was heading up the mountain.

Chapter 19
July – Plans

Over the weekend Mandy took the kids here, there and everywhere, buying ice creams, toys, visiting Nana, you name it they did it. It was what she needed to do to take her mind off what was staring at her in the face.

John was back to metal detecting and playing on computer games; nice John was gone and the bully was back. So, the more time out of the house the better and the kids were loving it.

The early intervention team had been in contact to arrange the final assessment for Dan and luckily it was next Wednesday before the meeting at the pub. This meeting could see them receiving an official diagnosis and enabling them to tap into more resources for her son. Having signed up for parenting classes so that she could learn how to be better for him, it was settling her worry about how he could be helped and the classes started in a few weeks.

Dan's differences and struggles were becoming more visible. During his occupational therapy assessment, they had discovered that he had spatial awareness and gross motor skill issues. So, things like ball sports were difficult for him because he couldn't work out where the ball was. He was a danger on a road as he couldn't see distance with cars, and he struggled with buttons, toileting and cutlery. Not the end of the world and all things that can be learned with lots of time and adaptations. But for now, it was about support for the little man.

Dan would always be perfect to her no matter what, just as Becca was.

Her train of thought was broken by a little voice.

'Mum, when Grandad dies, where will he go?' It was Becca.

Children have a knack of just saying what is in their head and Mandy believed that should be honoured with a truthful answer.

'He will go to heaven, Becca.'

'Will I be able to visit him there?'

'No, darling, he will be doing all the things he loves until we all join him again.'

'Can I still say my poem every night and God bless him?'

There was a real concern in her voice.

'I think that would be a lovely thing for you to do.'

'Mum.'

What was Dan going to ask? she wondered.

'Yes, Dan?'

'Can I have a choc ice?'

Mandy smiled. It was this pure innocence that had made her fight worthwhile, and that she loved this so much and never wanted to let go of it. No matter how hard things felt in the next few days, it was going to get sorted. She would never leave these two, never.

It was vital that a robust plan was created, meaning that there was work to do on Monday when the kids were at school. This needed to be sorted out once and for all and pride needed to be left at the door.

Monday arrived way too soon. John had calmed down a little but seemed to fixate on what this meant to him with all of this debt. Mandy didn't understand what he was getting at, because his name wasn't connected to the business.

Asking him to give her space to work, he obliged. With the kids off to school there was a full day to work on her plan. Her friend Doug, who was a financial adviser, was coming over at ten and they were going to brainstorm possible solutions. She was ready.

'So, option one is to set up payment plans with all of the suppliers and the brewery to clear the debt. This would be in the form of an IVA to cease the interest on the debts and would mean Angel is still operating the business and me overseeing it. This could take up to twenty years to clear based on the business profit and if she continues to do what she has done it could get worse,' Mandy summarised.

Doug nodded.

'That's correct, Mandy, and if the business fails you are still personally liable for the debt.'

'I don't like that plan. Option two is to use my settlement, borrow more to invest in the business, run it with Angel until the loan is repaid and the business is profitable.'

'I could find you a good rate,' Doug added.

'I just don't want to work in a pub, Doug.'

'Then you have to take option three, Mandy, it is the only way to do this. It won't be pleasant, I will give you that and rather you than me, but you are out of options.'

Mandy knew he was right but dreaded Thursday and beyond.

Chapter 20
July – D-Day

Thursday arrived and Mandy felt physically sick. Having dealt with equally bad situations like this in her job many times, it should be a piece of cake, but her sister wasn't part of the equation then.

As much as she was angry at Angel, she was still her little sister. "The black sheep" she was the one who cocked everything up, but still that little blond kid with the national health glasses who wasn't as smart and wasn't as pretty as her big sister, and Mandy felt partly responsible for her being the way she was. She had a lot to live up to and she just couldn't do it, no matter how many times she tried. Nobody had expected her to, she put the pressure on herself, everyone else just wanted her to be herself and live her life.

Sitting at the pub waiting when the area manager arrived, her gut was going again. There were a lot of entries in her diary over the last few weeks and today's entry would be a long one. Angel was being very cool with her, but much better than the previous week. She hadn't been to see their dad this week because she was "too stressed" with all this carry-on. Mandy wasn't biting. And she was looking forward to going to see her dad tomorrow.

The meeting convened. The area manager started to speak and said that he wanted to offer up his options and how the brewery could help them out.

Mandy stopped him.

'Look, David, I really appreciate how supportive, unfazed and honest you have been with us during the last few weeks. We couldn't have asked for more. However, I have come to a decision and it is not one that I have taken lightly. As you are aware, our dad is currently dying of cancer, this has put a lot of things into perspective for me and helped me to make decisions that I am comfortable with.'

'I understand, Mandy, continue,' David responded in a really supportive way.

'I have decided that we will apply for bankruptcy and work our months' notice as of today. I am aware that this will make Angel homeless and jobless, but it will also wipe out the debt. I am not taking this decision lightly as I have to declare all that I have and I will lose it. Angel has nothing so she has nothing to lose other than a roof over her head. She will commit to spending no more money and will use what stock is in the business and hand over all of the takings with no drawings for the next month and I will complete the application for business bankruptcy.'

Angel was bright red. Mandy could see that she was thinking, *What about me, poor me, how could you?* and so she was bracing herself for the eruption once David had gone. But for now, it was about formalities and paperwork. The screaming could wait.

Once David had left, a formal notice had been served and paperwork signed, Mandy closed the door and looked at Angel, waiting.

'You are making your own fucking sister and her family homeless, how could you? I hate you!' she screamed.

'My own sister spent almost one hundred thousand pounds that she didn't have and I am out of pocket here to the tune of around fifty thousand. Yet, I don't hate you.'

'You are so fucking smug, so far up your own arse, you think you are something and you are just a bitch. I am moving away and I never want to see you again. And if you think I am running this place for the next four weeks you've got another thing coming.'

Mandy hadn't planned for that last bit, needing her to do the right thing, but it was Angel, she would only do what suited her. Shit.

'Do you not feel any responsibility for this mess, Angel? Can you not see that you need to do the right thing here?' Mandy pleaded.

'No fucking way, it's not my fault I am depressed and I needed help and you didn't help me so it's your fault. I am going now so you better go on the bar, see how YOU like it.'

With that Angel stomped off.

There was no responding to her, she was so irrational, and had never been able to take responsibility. Shit.

What to do, what to do???

Then a thought came to her. There was her friend Lou who used to run a business for her many moons ago that was currently looking for work and she wondered if Lou would take on this difficult and awkward challenge. She would give her a call.

Chapter 21
August – Cavalry

It was Monday the third of August and Mandy had been at the pub all weekend running things, and realising just how bad it had been. The staff were unhappy, the punters were unhappy and there was a booze "on tick" list behind the bar and the local drunks were coming in asking for their beer on tick, and getting abusive when they were told no.

Thank goodness that Louise had agreed to run the pub for her. She had seen it as a great opportunity to let the brewery see how good she was and David had really liked her when they had been introduced. Mandy felt very grateful and humbled for such good friends and there were things in life more important than money.

Louise just rolled up her sleeves and got stuck in, sorting out the staff, working out how she would manage to make the best use of the current stock and working out a budget to spend for the next four weeks and agreeing that with David. Angel and Gareth did not make it easy for her; they would come down and eat the food out of the kitchen and help themselves to soft drinks, and when Louise challenged them, she would just get a mouthful of abuse. Mandy told her to just ignore it and write everything down and she would reimburse it to the business for the next four weeks.

It was difficult for Mandy to understand why her sister was so angry and so lacking in her ability to accept any responsibility for her actions. She had considered signing up for a psychology degree before her dad's condition had been diagnosed and now, she felt it would really help her to understand both her sister and her son. She had researched the modules on the open university website and she could study both child psychology and mental illness as part of the course so she was close to signing up but the biggest barrier was cost. She would ponder it a little longer.

This week's visit to Manchester had been difficult. Her dad was complaining of being too hot and that the nurses were not doing their jobs properly. In addition to this, there was the mafia conspiracy that was going on three beds down from him. He was confused and sitting with his notebook doing math again. Amy had been sickly sweet, trying to be best friends and Mandy had decided to be equally as nice in return so that in his last days her dad saw no conflict or negative feelings. In fact, Mandy had felt quite sorry for Amy. She was crying all of the time and worried about being alone, after all she was just a frail seventy-year-old woman facing the prospect of losing the man she loved, no matter how bad her behaviour had been towards her and her sister and at the end of the day all Mandy felt was empathy.

Louise called her to say that Angel had been down to the bar last night with Gareth, they had both gotten really drunk and had been slagging her off in the bar, to as many people who would listen. Mandy sighed deeply and apologised to Lou for her sister's behaviour and decided to go in and see her. But first, there was the job of completing the bankruptcy paperwork and that was a big task. Mandy was grateful that the auditors had identified all of the debt and listed it already. As part of the process, they both had the opportunity to also detail all personal debt, so she needed to meet with Angel and encourage her to be honest about her personal debt as well. Although she didn't have any herself, she had spoken to John and said that they could also write off any joint debt and she knew that there was a loan for his IT studies that had her name attached as guarantor so she had asked him to dig out the paperwork. He had been very sheepish and a bit off with her, but she put that down to his anger at Angel.

Everyone around her seemed to be angry at someone or something, it seemed such a useless emotion. None of them would feel better for it, it wouldn't solve anything, there was just no benefit to it and this was a great lesson to learn.

She gathered the paperwork and readied herself for going to see her sister, bracing herself for the storm.

Chapter 22
August – Agreement

Monday the tenth of August, the week had flown by and Mandy was on her way to see Angel to try and call a truce. They needed to finalise the bankruptcy paperwork and talk about Dad. Angel hadn't been to see him for two weeks because she had no money. She and Gareth had been to see the council and they wouldn't house them until they were actually homeless so they had asked the brewery to serve them with a section twenty-one which was taking time. They were both applying for jobs and were trying, so maybe there was a little bit of light at the end of the tunnel. In the meantime, they had both signed up for benefits but were waiting for their first payment. Mandy had three hundred pounds in an envelope to give them to tide them over, not really knowing why, but it was her sister so she justified her actions by convincing herself that Angel was family and needed her help.

Why did she always feel so responsible for her sister?

They had been close all of their lives and Mandy had always looked after Angel when their parents were working in the pubs, they were brought up in. But in trying to be like her big sis, Angel had constantly borrowed money and then struggled to pay it back. Job hopping and moving house more than anyone Mandy had ever known; Angel followed her all around the country wanting to be close to her. Mandy knew that Angel both idolised her and hated her and it wasn't her fault but she felt such a huge responsibility for her sister's failures and that is why she had bailed her out every time.

Her mum and dad had felt the same, only dad had got sick of it and given up, which had felt like abandonment to Angel. She had anchored herself to her family by constantly needing to be helped, being the little girl who had a tantrum every time she was told no and had learned some of the best emotional leverage techniques known to woman, she had skills after all.

The diary that Mandy had started when the cancer diagnosis had been revealed had evolved and was growing into a book. She was emptying her emotions, lessons and frustrations into it daily and had made the decision to have it published in memory of her dad when he had gone. It really was a great way of dealing with hurt, trauma, anger and analysing what was going on around you. Going back and reading how you had felt and what had happened just a few days ago was a reflective tool, almost like looking into a mirror at somebody else's life and having the ability to give them advice. She thought for a moment and recognised that this set of challenges was teaching her so many different lessons. She hoped that her actions were enough to win her life back and she was certainly giving it her all.

Deciding to just be kind and understanding to Angel and to offer her help, she set off to the pub.

It was obvious that Angel was ready for a fight, her body language was tense and her face taught. Mandy just went over to her and gave her a hug.

'I love you; you know. You are my little sister and you have screwed up but all I can do is to help you the best I can to get out of this mess.'

She could see Angel physically shrink and a look of relief come over her face. Then she cried, in fact, she sobbed.

'I am sorry, I am such a useless cow and I feel shit. I was so depressed that I wanted to die. Shopping and drinking were how I got through the day and I was too ashamed to ask for help. I thought you would all go mad at me and think I was useless. It turns out I am and everyone thinks that anyways,' Angel managed to say between sobs.

'I am not going to lie, everyone, including me is disappointed in you. Not because you have screwed up, but because you have done it again and you let it get so out of hand. But there is no point in being angry,' Mandy said softly but firmly.

'How can you not be angry with me?'

'Because there is no point to anger, where will it get us?'

Angel thought about that for a few minutes. She had spent most of her life angry at someone or something because she had been so bad at everything. Maybe Mandy had a point, it certainly felt good that she was not being shouted at or judged.

Eventually, words came to her again.

'So, what are we going to do?'

Mandy was calm, this was going well. Removing the anger from the situation and being honest in a supportive way was getting through, so keeping her voice at the same tone, she replied,

'That is the first time you have said we, so that is amazing progress, Sis, well done.'

She watched her sister sit up a little straighter.

'This does need to be a team approach so that the outcomes are the best they can be for all of us.'

Angel nodded enthusiastically.

'I have brought you some money to tide you over. I have completed the bankruptcy paperwork with all of the pub debts, but there is an opportunity here to write off all of our personal debt. Start from scratch with a clean slate. So, do you think you can be totally honest and get all of your paperwork together for everything you have?'

Angel sat forward in her seat, now totally engaged in the conversation.

'Yes, I can do that.'

'OK, when do you think you can do that by?'

'Tomorrow.'

'That would be great, our kid, then you will have an opportunity to start again with no baggage. There will be rules. You won't be able to have a car over the value of one thousand pounds, you can't take on any more debt for six years and if you come into any money it has to go to the official receiver to allocate against the debt. Does that make sense?'

'Yes, sort of. Can I keep any money I earn or do I have to hand some of it over?' Angel said looking worried.

This was such good progress; Mandy couldn't remember the last time that they had managed a proper conversation. Removing the anger had really paid dividends.

'No, you don't have to hand anything over. You need to learn to live on what you earn. You will have to go to your bank, they will close your account and you need to open a basic bank account, but you still get a debit card and can have benefits or wages paid into it. It is only if you came into a lump sum that you would have to hand it over, like a tax rebate or something similar,' Mandy explained, keeping her voice soft and positive.

'Is it the same rules for you?' Angel actually looked remorseful again, which meant she was learning.

'Yes, I will lose everything and, like you, I will have to learn to live on what I have and have an old banger for a car. We will be totally equal, so you have the same chance as me to turn your life around. Please try and do something positive with this, Angel, it really is a clean slate and a chance to start again. If I can forgive and forget, then surely you can?'

Angel leaned over and gave her sister a hug.

'I am going to try,' she said, and that was that.

Angel knew what she had to do; she had her deadline so they had a plan.

'Do you want to come down with me on Thursday to see Dad?' Mandy asked.

'Yes please, I would love that.'

'Then I will pick you up at seven-thirty and we will head straight off. Dad said he was really hot last week so I am going to buy him a fan for his bedside. I will see you Thursday morning; if you have all your paperwork ready by then I will finish everything off and submit it on Friday. Remember to include everything!'

'I will see you then, Sis,' Angel responded.

Mandy left with her heart a little fuller. This was good. The NLP and life coaching she had been studying had really helped her to deal with this situation. Maybe the law of attraction was in play here and she was attracting into her life the tools she needed in order to deal with the problems that she was facing. Having completed both courses really quickly by using every hour she had available and then being awarded a distinction for both, she had been really pleased with herself. It turns out that if you really set your mind to it you can do anything, so she had promptly signed up for another Diploma in Building Self Confidence, as this would give her a really robust tool kit to enable her to help others. Still undecided about the psychology degree, this was enough for now. What had become evident was that learning new things was filling up some of the empty and negative space that losing her job and having problems in her marriage had left, so moving forward with more of the same seemed like a good option.

Was this part of the challenge? Learning how to balance the bad things by taking on positive self development activities, only time would tell. So, she set off for home in a pensive mood and looked forward to seeing the two beautiful faces that made every day worthwhile.

Today's entry into her diary would have a lot of learning in it.

Chapter 23
August – Fan

Despite Amy trying to convince them not to go down, they were going anyway.

Mandy arrived a few minutes before seven-thirty on Thursday the thirteenth of August to collect Angel and drive to Manchester to see the man they loved so much. The feeling of fear and dread that came every week on visit day was bubbling in her gut and she felt sick. *How would he be today?* she wondered.

Angel opened the door at that moment and broke her train of thought.

'Morning, Sis,' she said as she plonked herself in the passenger seat.

'Morning, our kid, how are you feeling today about going to see Dad?' Mandy asked her, noticing that her eyes were puffy and red so she had obviously been crying.

'I can't stop crying,' Angel responded, confirming Mandy's suspicions.

'Because of Dad or the pub?'

'Just Dad; now that I have slept on it, I think we are doing the right thing with the pub and yesterday you were brilliant. You are my hero you, know.'

She seemed genuine.

'I am just doing what needs to be done.'

'No, it's more than that. You are so strong, practical and calm; I couldn't do what you have done in a million years. But the fact that it is organised and we have a plan has given me time to think about Dad. We are going to lose him, really soon, aren't we?' tears were streaming down her face when she said this.

Mandy was struggling to keep her voice from wobbling when she replied,

'We have whatever time we have, our kid; we need him to see us happy and positive. We need to tell him we love him and that we will see him next week and that is all we can do. As for time, none of us knows. We could be hit by a lorry on the motorway and be gone before him, so let's pull ourselves together,

70

think of all of those weekends in Blackpool with his kiss me quick hat and be what he needs today.'

Angel nodded and wiped her face.

'I think I can do that.'

'That's the spirit, so let's go, and I will try to avoid dodgy-looking lorries.'

Angel smiled and they set off talking about their funny, cuddly and lovely Dad.

The last couple of days at home had been testing. John had been extremely sheepish and out a lot. Becca was asking lots of questions about Grandad and death and if Mum was going to divorce Dad.

Where had she got that from? Had John said something or was she picking up on his behaviour?

Dan has settled down a lot since he was going to occupational therapy every week and having some counselling assessment. He really liked the lady he was seeing and they were working on a project about self-esteem which seemed to be really improving things for him. The school had also been great, there had been three meetings with all of the parties involved and a plan for how they could do the best for Dan had been implemented. He was learning basic skills at occupational therapy like doing up zips and buttons, and wiping his bum; this was actually quite funny because they were using a plastic bum and chocolate spread so Dan would no longer eat it. He wasn't making much progress here though, he just couldn't manage any of these things easily, even using a knife and fork was hard for him, but Mandy didn't want to make any of them into a big thing for the time being because they were the least of her worries.

Becca was wise beyond her years at nine. Mandy called her the "Why Bird" because she asked so many questions all of the time. She was incredibly beautiful and a talented dancer, having started ballet aged three in her little tutu. She now did ballet, tap, modern, jazz and anything else she could do that was dance related. It cost a fortune and saw Mandy travelling the ten miles into Alnwick for seven classes a week sitting with all the "dance mums" she felt that she was definitely not one of them. It did cross her mind that they would struggle with the dance fees after the bankruptcy as all of her money and assets were gone, but she would worry about that when it happened.

Her mind had drifted to thinking about her home life and she had obviously driven on autopilot to the motorway, quickly pulling herself around because the last time that happened, she had an accident. Angel had put some rock music on for her so they were feeling a little more upbeat.

'I bought a top of the range fan for Dad, it's on the back seat.'

Angel looked over to check it out.

'Oooooo fancy, I am sure he will love that,' she oozed.

The drive was long, over four hours, because traffic was slow with morning jams and speed calmed areas, but they arrived at the hospital just before midday.

When they made it to the ward there were no nurses to be seen, so they just headed to their dad's bed.

The sight that greeted them would be forever etched into Mandy's brain. Their precious dad, this once big powerful man with his jolly Santa laugh and a sense of fun never matched by anyone before or since, was sitting on a commode at the side of his bed, curtain open so everyone could see, with his underpants around his ankles, crying because he couldn't move. Shame and embarrassment were written all over his face.

What happened next would also stay with Mandy forever. Her failure of a sister, the black sheep, the one who constantly screwed up, just rushed over to him, scooped him up, placed him on the bed, closed the curtain and cleaned him up and made him decent. In that one act of kindness that restored her beloved dad's dignity, Angel had redeemed herself in her sisters' eyes from every wrong she had ever done.

It was no more than four minutes of time, but it had passed in slow motion and had immobilised her whilst her sister had taken action.

With eyes full, and heart even fuller, Mandy placed the new fan on one her dad's bedside cabinet, kissed him on the head, sat in the visitor's chair opposite her sister and looked at them both grateful for this moment.

He was weak. He must have been no more than eight stone, less than half his normal weight.

But he looked at them both holding one of their hands in each of his and just said, 'My girls.'

It was a loving visit, some laughing, some quiet while Dad drowsed and some emotional moments. But the three of them were held together in this one hour of time. It was almost as if a glorious aura had surrounded them and Mandy could feel the presence of Grandad waiting, holding out his arms in a welcome gesture. It was beautiful.

As they drove away from the hospital that day on the thirteenth of August, Mandy felt that she would never see her dad again. She had planned to go the following week, but her gut was playing up again.

Dismissing it as just upset from the visit she turned to Angel and said, 'Thank you for what you did there, it was like it was the most natural thing in the world for you to do. I know you have done a bit of caring before, but have you ever thought about doing it again? You would be really good at it.'

Angel smiled and said, 'I hadn't, but maybe I should, it felt natural for me as well, he just needed help and I was there, that was all.'

'Don't ever undermine what you just did, it was an act of pure love and kindness, and the look of gratitude and love in dad's eyes was something I wish I could have bottled for you to look at every day. I know you guys have been in a bad place for the last few years, thanks to the step monster, but that all melted away in that moment.'

Angel wept.

So did Mandy.

They wept and grieved together for this man that was such a huge role model to them and an influence on them, and they knew that those days were gone, and all that they could do now was be there for him as often as they could until the end.

The fan had made his day and he wouldn't let them turn it off. He was comfortable and he had his dignity. They had given him that today.

Chapter 24
August – Shock

Back to reality with a bang.

Friday the fourteenth of August, bankruptcy completion day. Angel had declared everything and handed the paperwork over the previous day. There were an additional thirteen thousand pounds of personal debt, but Mandy was beyond shock now, or so she thought.

John had shuffled up to the dining room table once the kids were shipped off to Nanas, with his pile of paperwork.

He still looked sheepish and Mandy wondered what was going on and what he was about to tell her.

'Look, you need to understand that it was really hard being at home on my own when you were out at work all day, I got bored and I ended up buying things for my computer,' he managed to stutter out.

'OK, like what?' Mandy replied inquisitively.

'Games, new parts, upgrades, graphics cards, stuff like that.'

'So, what are you saying?' she urged.

'Well I took out a couple of credit cards in your name because I couldn't get one,' he blurted.

'You did what?'

Actually, feeling a bit stunned, Mandy couldn't help shouting. After all she had just been through with Angel, she really didn't expect to be doing it again. *Maybe it was just a small amount,* she thought, but her gut was telling her otherwise. Feeling tense and bracing herself once again for the punch line, she wondered how far away she was from her loved ones and their actions for failing to notice all of this. Working a lot of hours had been a part of her job, but it had allowed them a good lifestyle, so why was everyone around her getting into debt, or so it seemed?

Turning to John, she took a deep breath and waited.

A couple of minutes passed while John studied his feet and plucked up courage, but silence was the card she chose to play.

'Well I have the loan for the study course and there are about four thousand pounds left on that to pay, the credit cards come to another twelve thousand five hundred pounds and I am overdrawn at the bank by six hundred pounds,' he eventually said.

'Over seventeen thousand pounds that I knew nothing about, you must have been really bloody bored!'

She needed to get out, some fresh air, a walk, anything just to try and clear her head and think about this challenge. This one could be tricky because there was more to it than just debt. She knew it had not been computer parts and equipment that he had spent so much money on.

'Well I need a bit of thinking time, John, obviously, this can be written off but there is now a trust issue, so I think I just need to take a walk with the dogs. Leave the paperwork on the table and I will look at it when I get back,' was all she could manage to say.

The urge to hit him over the head with the damn paperwork was strong so removing herself quickly was best for both of them.

'Do you want to talk about it again or can I go out?'

Through gritted teeth, she managed, 'You can go.'

Being outside in nature and playing with the dogs was a real tonic. What to do? What to do? This wasn't just about the money, that could be written off. This was about John, who had lied, fraudulently used her details to obtain credit and obviously spent it on whoever he was having an affair with. This was more than just including the debt in the bankruptcy paperwork, although she would do that, it was a big decision. One she really didn't want to make.

Not because she didn't want to leave the marriage, but because she didn't want to be the bad guy in the kid's eyes. Over the last few weeks, Becca had been asking a lot whether Mum and Dad were going to get divorced, and she had constantly reassured Becca that it would not happen. How could she tell them that the marriage was over and it was she who wanted to leave? Would they ever understand that? This was going to be a really tough challenge, because who knew what the right outcome was for all of them?

What if she chose to stay and that was the wrong choice for the challenge? Her life would be over and her beloved children would be stuck with their idiot father. What if she chose to leave and that was the wrong choice for the challenge? They might hate her for it, and they would still end up with their idiot father! This was too much for her brain to deal with. For now, she decided to sleep on it, but do the paperwork and send it off anyway.

Thank goodness for the kids and the dogs, they loved her no matter what and were happy with just her love.

Chapter 25
August – Confession

It was Saturday morning and human children and furry children were up with the larks as usual. Mandy was busy making pancakes with two helpers on the workbenches who were making a mess and with two on the kitchen floor waiting for any fallout. There were berries, chopped banana and lashings of maple syrup ready to be poured over the steaming pancakes as they came out of the griddle pan.

'I can eat nine!' exclaimed Becca.

'Well, I can eat twelve,' Dan countered.

Making pancakes three at a time had helped a lot with their timetables, but not a lot with their appetite for pancakes because at ages nine and four, they could manage more than the average adult if left unsupervised. They were damn good though, she had to admit to herself.

John had been very late back last night and was still in bed as usual. It was customary for him to remain in bed until after one whenever she had a day off, so this was no exception. Mandy loved it and would always have the kids full of pancakes and into town for dance lessons, shopping and beach visits with the dogs on the way home before John had even properly awoken.

He was missing so much of their lives, in fact so much of life in general.

However, she felt indifferent to him and to both of those facts right now, it was his choice.

It was his choice!

By going to dance lessons and to the beach, there was time to reflect and ask what she wanted. Maybe if she just trusted the universe then John would be forced into making the choice. She would wait it out and see what happened. He was obviously with the new woman last night so maybe it wouldn't take long.

The sound of barking and laughing drew her attention back to the kids and dogs. Here was her world, right in front of her. Sitting on the white sandy beach of Sugar Sands, with the cool crisp breeze tousling her hair, she watched them all playing together. Kids running into the sea, screaming and running out again and the dogs were chasing the sticks that were being thrown for them and they were barking excitedly. It was a picture of pure innocence and happiness. No matter how bad things were elsewhere, this was bliss. It was a shame they didn't live closer to the beach, because it would be a real joy to do this more often.

When they arrived home, it was after two and everyone was ready for a snack and a rest. With their lunch eaten Becca went to play with her dolls and Dan went for a nap.

John couldn't have been up for more than half an hour when they arrived home and he was sitting in the living room looking worse for wear when she walked in with her coffee.

'You were late back last night,' she said nonchalantly.

'Yesterday freaked me out a bit so I needed some thinking time,' was his reply.

'Really, and what conclusion did you reach, if any?'

'I have something to tell you and I don't want you to freak out,' he replied.

'Spit it out then,' was all she could muster.

'I... I...I...' he stuttered.

'For goodness sake just say it,' she said with impatience.

'I have met somebody else.'

At last he had said it.

She felt absolutely overjoyed but tried not to look like that. This had been even quicker than she had imagined, what an absolute result. But even as the thought entered her head, she felt a wave of sadness. They had been together for thirteen years, and had produced two amazing children, how could she feel so indifferent? They had drifted apart over the years, his bullying and angry behaviour coupled with his laziness had made her dislike him. The more she had disliked him, the more hours she had worked to stay away from him. Then she had felt guilty for also being away from the kids but knew the quality of her time with them and the amount she did for them was far greater than anything he could ever do.

'So, what do you want to do? Your timing is not the best with my dad being ill and the bankruptcy, as well as Dan's diagnosis status and with me having lost my job?'

'I know, and I don't know what I want to do yet. I won't leave until there is progress with your dad and the bankruptcy is sorted, but I don't want to be married anymore.'

It felt like him offering to stay for a bit was his way of appearing to still be a good guy, which was laughable really, but she played along.

'OK, let's park it for now and deal with everything else first and then talk about a plan in a few weeks. I am not surprised you know, and I can be a grown-up so I won't make it difficult,' she assured him.

'Are you not fucking bothered? You don't give a shit about me, do you? You never even asked me if I would think about it, you are a fucking bitch!!!'

Now that she hadn't expected. He seemed genuinely aggrieved that she had not tried to convince him to stay. How could he be the one having an affair and then blame her for not caring?

Maybe he had a point in a way though. The only thing that had mattered to her over the last couple of years had been the kids and her job. Perhaps he had felt neglected and unloved, like many women do when their men work all of the time. Saying that, she still did all of the woman's chores, was the finance manager, the main childcare provider and cook, so it wasn't exactly the same as the role reversal situation. There were no nights out drinking, boy's activities or mistresses like men have; she had no life but work and kids, so really, she should not be feeling sorry for him. He was always full of "poor me" and would never take any responsibility so she was not going to let herself be taken down that road.

'There is no need to shout and I don't think you have a right to be angry with me. I am trying to be practical. I had an inkling that there was something going on, your revelation about the credit cards confirmed it, and when I checked your credit card spending you DID NOT spend the money on ONLY the items you told me about, did you?'

That had shut him up.

Mandy had phoned the credit card companies and requested an online pin so she could view statements, not a problem as they were in her name. She had chuckled to herself when the hotel and restaurant purchases had pinged up. New ladies clothing, flowers, jewellery and the occasional pc game had confirmed all of her suspicions.

'I am sorry, I don't know why it happened, I was just lonely.'

'Well it has, and I would just appreciate a bit of respect and planning time. There is no reason for us to be anything but amicable for the sake of the kids. You can go out as often as you like, but do not spend money you don't have because if you create any more debt then it leaves with you. Think yourself lucky that I haven't called the police and had you arrested for fraud.'

On that note, she went upstairs to play dolls with Becca and let any thought of John leave her head. She had chosen her children over her husband, it felt like the right choice and no challenge at all.

Chapter 26
August – Family

John had disappeared and never returned after their discussion, which made Mandy very happy indeed. She had stayed up late with the kids watching Disney movies and eating homemade popcorn. They had donned headlamps and walked the dogs in the dark making it a spooky adventure and she had allowed them all to pile in her bed for the night. *Sod him,* she thought to herself, if he does come home, he can sleep elsewhere.

He didn't.

They all awoke when Jet jumped on the bed and landed in the middle of them. He wasn't the smallest black Labrador in the world and once he was up Ozzy soon followed with the grace of a gazelle, as collies tend to have.

Jet had been Becca's seventh Birthday gift and they had brought the little eight-week-old puppy home and he had stolen their hearts. After he had turned one, Mandy thought he needed some company and just as she had been thinking about it, her cousin had posted a picture on Facebook of the most adorable Border Collie that had been abandoned and needed a home. It was love at first sight and he joined the family a week later. He was to be "Dan's" dog so that they both had their own and Ozzy was destined to be the very tonic that Dan needed to help him out with his autism journey.

Having never had a Labrador or a Collie before this was learning for Mandy. The loyalty and affection that Jet brought to the family and the intelligence of Ozzy, taught them all something new every day. For bedtime stories, they gave Mandy content for her creative mind to come up with adventures that included the kids and the dogs, and Super Jet and Super Ozz were born, with their special owners Becca and Dan who would discover their own superpowers and regularly save the world, well their local town initially. These stories would prove to be such an amazing tool in building Dan's confidence and allowing him to see his autism as a superpower rather than a negative condition.

All things happen for a reason, she thought to herself.

Picking up the phone as the kids got dressed, she called her mum.

'Hi, Mum, do you fancy a few hours at the beach with the kids today? The weather is gorgeous and they had such a great time yesterday. They have been mithering me all morning, plus with all that is going on with Dad, I would really like to spend some time with you.'

Mandy had been thinking a lot about her mum since her dad had been diagnosed. Although she made a point of going to see her every week, it was just popping in for no more than an hour on a Saturday while the kids were at dance lessons and she couldn't remember the last time that she had made time to do something a bit more meaningful.

Rita responded with such a delighted tone.

'I would love that; shall I make a nana picnic?'

'I don't think that you would get a single negative response to that question, I won't be able to contain the kids when I tell them that you are making a picnic!' she laughed, knowing that there would be lots of food and in particular, cake.

'I will pick you up in about an hour or so, is that OK?' she asked.

'That will be perfect, I can sort Ray out with his dinner before I abandon him,' her mum replied.

Ray was the man that her mum had an affair with which broke up the twenty-five-year marriage to her dad. To be fair, she had not been happy with her dad and Ray was a nice enough man and a reasonable stepdad, considerably better than the step monster, Amy. He made her mum so much happier than she had been with their dad, so both Mandy and Angel had accepted him easily.

However, he was a typical Northumbrian man and really could not fend for himself, so every outing had to be managed around mealtimes so that his food could be prepared and instructions left in advance. Mandy chuckled at the thought; Angel and her had never really understood why their mum put him on such a pedestal and tended to his every need, but they knew that she was a carer and a feeder and she couldn't help it.

Whatever made her happy, Mandy thought. She knew only too well how it felt to be in a marriage that was desperately unhappy.

With very excited children and dogs safely packed into the car, she set off to her mum's house, leaving no note for John and feeling full of joy to be spending time with people she loved so much.

They had collected Nana and the largest quantity of food that could be packed into a picnic basket and were singing "wheels on the bus" en route to Sugar Sands.

The sun was blazing with just enough of a cool breeze to make it comfortable. Sugar Sands was the best-kept secret in the local village near to her mum and they loved going because they were four of only twelve people on this vast white sandy beach with a crystal-clear blue sea. Perfection.

With the picnic laid out, and what a spread, Becca and Dan were running around half-naked covered in factor fifty and in their elements. Sandwich in one hand, cake in the other and a greedy Labrador chasing the food waiting for a morsel to drop, Mandy sat watching them with her mum.

'This is lovely, isn't it? We don't often get the chance to spend time together like this,' Mandy said.

'It is lovely, and I am so pleased you asked, I love watching Becca and Dan running around like this. Can I ask if everything is alright with you and John?'

How do mums just know? It never ceased to amaze Mandy that she could go for ages not seeing her mum properly and not really telling her anything and yet she still knew what was going on.

'Not really, Mum.'

She paused and then decided to just tell her everything about the debt, his behaviour and the other woman.

'I never liked him; you know. The first time you brought him to meet us, I thought he was nowhere near good enough for you. He is an idiot; he is stupid and you can do so much better.'

Well, of course, her mum was going to say that, but it made her feel good and loved anyway.

'Thanks, Mum, I knew you would understand,' Mandy said gratefully.

'So, what are you going to do?' Rita asked, looking concerned.

'Nothing immediately. With Dad being so ill, the bankruptcy, Dan's assessments, treatments and classes, I think we just need to hold off for a few weeks. But it will only be weeks as I don't think I can bear him to be around me for much longer. And at least I can tell the kids that it was him, which is a relief for me.'

'He is the biggest idiot on God's green earth, throwing away this beautiful family, but you will all be better off without him,' her mum replied.

Mandy agreed with that! She was actually looking forward to it just being her and the kids and couldn't imagine ever wanting to be with another man again, she had enough now.

Turning to her mum she reached over, took hold of a seventy-year-old, wrinkled, freckled bony hand and said, 'I am so pleased that we are spending this quality time. Facing the prospect of losing Dad has reminded me of how precious you are and I would like to do this more often. I love you, Mum; you have been an absolute angel in all of my life, thank you.'

A tear trickled down her mum's face. They had never been a lovey-dovey family, not really hugging or expressing themselves. That is why Mandy had done the exact opposite with her children; they hugged, kissed and said I love you all of the time, but it was a lot harder to say those words to her mum. Not today though, the words came easy, were heartfelt and obviously had an impact.

Trying to compose herself, Rita replied, 'You have made me proud every single day of your life, I love you very much and I trust that whatever you decide to do next, that it will be the right thing. Let the guide that I know who is there for you lead the way, I feel you are on a path.'

That actually took Mandy's breath away. How could her mum know what was happening, or did she know? Was she just being generic and telling her to trust herself? Whatever the message was it hit home and they hugged until a large wet dog landed beside them and decided to shake the North Sea all over the picnic.

Chapter 27
August – Home

Sunday melted away with bubble baths, take away for dinner and cuddles on the couch. Monsters Inc. was the backdrop to winding down and tonight, Super Jet and Super Ozz saved the community from impending doom by re-directing an asteroid which was heading directly towards them. Thank goodness for their amazing superpowers and Super Dan was instrumental in the heroic actions that saved the village, which the mayor and local people were eternally grateful for, as always.

'Where's, Dad?' Becca asked.

'He has been at some sort of metal detecting event, so I am not sure what time he is getting back, love,' Mandy lied.

Not convinced, Becca replied, 'You and Dad are not getting divorced, are you?'

'What makes you ask that, darling?' Mandy probed.

'Well, Dad has not been very nice lately and you seem very upset.'

'I am upset about my dad, darling, and I can't say why your dad is behaving in that way. I will always be here for you no matter what happens in the future,' she tried to reassure her daughter.

'As long as I have you, Mum, I don't like my dad.'

A bit taken aback, Mandy steadied herself and engaged her brain before speaking.

'What makes you say that, Becca?'

'When you are at work, he shouts at us all the time, plays on his computer and never does anything with us. I sit in my room on my own and always want to phone you but I know you are busy.'

The rage came quickly, the tears followed but she managed to hold them both back. She needed to find out more and she really needed to be calm.

'Tell me what that feels like?' she managed, engaging all of her best leadership and coaching skills to ask the right questions.

'Well, it makes me really sad. Then I feel mad and want to kick my dad, especially when he is shouting at Dan. He shouts really loud and gets really angry if we interrupt his game. Dan just stays quiet and plays on his games. He even hit Ozzy last week and that made me really hate him,' she revealed.

'But I am not working now, Becca, I know I have been out visiting my dad and dealing with some stuff, but I am here more.'

Becca burst into tears and said she loved her mum being there and didn't want her to leave them with Dad anymore.

Mandy's heart just about broke in two. When she had gone back to work after maternity leave, it was with confidence that she was leaving her beloved children in the right hands, with their father. It had been the hardest thing she had ever had to do because she longed to be home with them but knew she could provide the best life for them in her highly paid job, so back to work she went and they would never want anything. How wrong can you be? Now they were going to lose everything anyway, thanks to the greed and actions of two people who were supposed to be family, who were supposed to have her back. Vowing there and then that she would do absolutely anything to keep her children from knowing how bad things were, she would pretend everything was the same and work out the "how" later.

Laying down on the bed with Becca she cuddled her until she fell asleep and then kissed Dan who was already fast asleep. She crept downstairs, just as John was creeping in the back door.

'The kids are asleep, so don't make any noise,' she said curtly.

'What the fuck is up with you? You said it was OK for me to go out, you know the deal. You having one of your huffs again?'

'No, I just can't be bothered with you, so make yourself a bed somewhere other than in my bed and be quiet,' she responded and there was a definite "just fucking do it" tone to her voice.

John complied and said nothing more.

Just as she has sprinkled a spoon of coffee into her mug and the kettle clicked off the phone rang. Rushing to answer so as not to wake the kids she was there in seconds.

'Hello,' she whispered.

'Hi, Mandy, it's me, Amy, I am phoning to let you know that they are bringing your dad home tonight because it's where he wants to be.' Amy's voice grated on her, but she checked her thoughts and centred them on her dad.

'That sounds like a positive action then, does that mean he is a little stronger?' Mandy inquired.

'Yes, he is adamant he will be better if he is at home.'

'Perfect, I think we will come down on Tuesday then, is that OK with you?'

'I suppose so, he doesn't really want visitors, but I suppose as long as you don't stay long that will be fine.' Amy whined.

Fury was bubbling again, but Mandy contained it for the millionth time this month, thanked Amy then hung up the phone.

Immediately, she called Angel to update her and ask if she wanted to come.

'Yes, I want to come and so does Nathan.'

Nathan was Angel's eldest son and Mandy was very close to him so she had agreed that it was fine. They had chatted for about ten minutes about how they were feeling and then said goodnight, quite civilly really, but Mandy felt like there was a rumbling beneath the surface and readied herself for whatever the next challenge would be.

At this moment in time everything felt like a test, every conversation, every twist and turn of events, it felt never-ending. But she knew she had to stay strong and keep going no matter what.

Chapter 28
August – Nathan

Tuesday the eighteenth of August, 7.30 a.m. and Mandy was sitting outside the pub waiting for Angel and Nathan to get into the car. She had spoken to Louise the previous day to check in on how things were going and Lou had updated her on the horror stories. Angel had been moody and all over the place, Gareth was drunk daily, Nathan and Jack, Angel's youngest son, just looked confused but Lou was doing her best and the brewery were happy with her and had offered her the pub to manage on a twelve-month contract after Angel and Gareth had moved out and she had ripped their hand off.

She was pleased for Louise, she was a hard worker and a good friend, it was just a shame that she was caught in the middle at the minute. Strength and resilience were two of her friend's best skills, so she wasn't too concerned about her.

Angel and Nathan settled into the car and they set off on the eight-hour round trip in the hopes that Amy would grant them enough time with their dad to make it a worthwhile journey.

'How are you feeling about seeing Grandad, Nath?' Mandy asked her nephew.

Nathan was still young and quite immature at eighteen years old. He had lived with her and John for six months when he wasn't getting along with his mum and there was still a bit of animosity on Angel's part about that. He had been a joy to have, Mandy had set ground rules that he had never had before and spent hours talking to him, teaching him and secretly coaching him to build his self-esteem.

Angel was not always the best mum, Mandy had witnessed her anger with them and spoken to her sister more than once, never sure if she was really listening. The usual response was a "poor me" one, with, "You don't know how hard it is," or, "It's OK for you, you have everything," guilt trip. Nathan and Jack were good boys and Mandy had spent many a sleepless night worrying about how they were being treated.

Angel had made some bad choices in men as well, and Mandy wasn't sure how they had treated her boys, it had been one of the biggest worries of her life. When Nathan had asked if he could come and stay with them, both her and John had readily said yes despite space being limited, they had found a way for this beautiful boy. They both loved him dearly.

Nathan responded and re-focused her thoughts, 'I am quite nervous actually, but I really want to see Grandad.'

'I think he will be really happy to see you, Nath, and he needs every bit of happiness we can bring at the minute. Let's just hope that he is feeling a bit chirpier than the last time me and your mum saw him.'

'Thanks for letting me come, Auntie Mandy, it's good to see you as well.'

It had been a surprise when Nathan had decided to move back to his mum's, and Mandy had wondered at the time what the reason was, but never questioned him. It had been just before his grandad's diagnosis, so she pondered as to whether it had anything to do with John's behaviour and his affair. Maybe Nathan had found out and not wanted to be in the middle of it. Of course, he wouldn't say anything because he would want to protect her, but it niggled.

She really loved both her nephews and her niece and trusted that one day, Angel would be the mum that they needed.

They spent the car journey reminiscing, as usual, talking openly about the man they were on their way to see. It was heart-breaking and uplifting.

The diary that Mandy had started had gained a title "Cancer Diary of a Daughter", she decided to have it published and had found a self-publishing house. The royalties would go to Cancer Research and it would be her tribute to her dad. It was the only bit of control that she felt she had in his demise. Having decided to speak to Amy today about what plans were in place, she also intended to ask if Amy needed any financial help. But the reason for doing this was to explore options in at least having a little input into her dad's send-off when it did happen.

Not if, when.

It was so painful to be thinking that way, but it was a fact they may only have a couple of months now, judging by the state of him last time her and Angel had visited, so practicalities had to be considered. It was encouraging however that he was home, surely, they would not allow him to go home unless he was much improved.

The road seemed longer every visit, she just wanted to get there and wished there was a quicker way. It felt urgent today for some reason. Her lovely dad. How could it be? It just wasn't fair; he was only sixty-seven. She often had moments where this wave of "it's not fair" took over her. She felt it wasn't allowed because of her test. Her challenge was to be strong because if she wasn't, she might fail and lose it all, but some days she just wanted to curl up in a corner and cry for hours on end. She didn't have that luxury. She must keep going and she MUST find the strength.

Oh, how easy it would be to be Angel who just gave up when things were hard, then someone came along and bailed you out. But, NO, she could not let her mind be taken in that direction because in that direction was anxiety, depression, hopelessness and weakness. She never had been weak, manipulative and a failure, yet she was currently about to fail in an epic manner.

She would lose every penny of her savings, her severance, her car, in fact, everything of any value. She would be a single mum having failed at marriage, yet again. She had failed at work and lost the career she loved.

No, just no. You will not allow your mind to wander like that. Why was this happening today? It happened occasionally, but she could usually nip it immediately, but today she kept drifting.

'How are you feeling, Auntie Mandy?' Nathan asked.

It was like he knew. They were connected. *Thank you, Nathan, I needed that,* she thought.

'I am feeling sad, Nath. You probably need to prepare yourself for what you are about to see. It won't be easy, he looks terrible, he has lost a lot of weight and it is a shock,' she replied, grateful for the interaction.

'Mum said he looked terrible, so I have kind of tried to imagine it, but I keep seeing happy, jolly Grandad,' Nathan responded.

'He will try to be, for you, I can guarantee that.'

Next turn Sale. They were near. It was gut-wrenching. *Stay strong, Mandy. Keep your focus.*

The car pulled up outside the house. His house. The curtains were drawn in the bedroom window so she knew where he was.

'Come on then, let's get this over with,' she said in such an upbeat manner.

She actually didn't recognise herself speaking.

Chapter 29
August – Bacon

It was just before lunchtime as they walked into her dad's house. Well in actual fact it was "Amy's" house, a fact that she had constantly humiliated her dad about when in front of others.

When Brian King had left his mega salary, tax-free job in the middle east to retire, he had been an idiot with his money and had no pension provision and no property after he had split up with Mum and had no idea how to budget. He was in need of another woman in order to survive so when Amy tootled along, he snapped her up. She had a house.

So, in order to keep him firmly in his place, Amy felt like she had the right to mention her house and his lack of pension at every opportunity. One of the many, many reasons she was difficult to like. Mandy shuddered and continued into the chintz palace that smelled of pungent lavender. Angel and Nathan followed closely behind.

'How is he?' Mandy asked Amy as they were ushered into the living room.

'He is very weak today, and not really keen on having visitors, so you need to keep it fairly brief,' was the reply that she had totally expected to hear. 'Do you want a cup of tea before you go up?' she added.

'That would be lovely, thank you, Amy.'

Angel shot her a "what the fuck" glance, but she ignored her and gave Amy their orders.

When the step monster left the room, Mandy turned to Angel and said, 'Be polite, I have my reasons, there are things I want to find out.'

'Oh, I see, but I can't stand her and don't really want to talk to her.'

Nathan piped up, 'Mum, just be nice, she will be sad as well, you know, even if you don't like her.'

Well said, Nathan, Mandy thought to herself.

Just then Amy appeared at the door with a tray of tea, milk and sugar. No biscuits though and they were all starving, it had been a long morning with lots of traffic jams so they hadn't stopped.

But just as that thought entered her head Amy said, 'Would you all like a bacon sandwich?'

'That sounds amazing, you don't mind, do you?' Mandy responded, ever so politely, being very mindful of her tone and manner.

'Well, have your tea and go and see your dad, then I will have your sandwiches ready when you come down,' Amy replied.

Whilst drinking tea, Mandy managed to steer the conversation around to plans.

'I know it is not something any of us wants to even consider, but have you thought about funeral plans and do you need any help? I would love to write a eulogy and read it,' Mandy managed to get in.

'Oh no!' exclaimed Amy.

It was like she had just been slapped in the face.

'Your dad was adamant about nobody speaking at his funeral and everything else has been sorted. We went to a funeral last year and there were four people who stood up and read out eulogies and your dad thought they were probably a load of hypocrites and said he didn't want every Tom, Dick and Harry standing up at his funeral telling a load of lies.'

'Well, I am not every Tom, Dick and Harry, am I? I am his daughter who is very close to him,' Mandy responded assertively.

'No, no, no,' Amy burst into tears, 'your dad said no, so that is how it has to be. He changed his will as well and left everything to me, he insisted. It is up to him after all. Anyway, you better go up now and I will make your sandwiches.'

They trooped upstairs with Angel poking Mandy in the back.

'Not now,' Mandy hissed, 'wait until we are in the car, smile and keep it in.'

The three of them entered the overkill chintz bedroom and in the middle of the bed looking small and insignificant was their dad and grandad, trying his best to produce a big beaming smile.

'Hi, Dad,' Mandy said when what she really wanted to say was, 'Oh my fucking God!'

'Hello, all of you, it's lovely to see you all,' he managed to say, but it felt like hard work.

He looked like death. That was the only way that she could describe it. He had no colour; he was even thinner and breathing looked like hard work.

'It's lovely to see you too, Dad,' she managed, as did Angel and Nathan. 'How're things?'

'They are as well as they can be, I'm not getting any younger or fitter, am I? I am struggling with most things, but Rita is looking after me well.'

They exchanged looks but didn't say a word. Did he know he had just called Amy, Rita, obviously not? It didn't matter, it was actually comforting because Mandy knew that it didn't matter who he was married to, he would only ever love Rita Harper, their mum and his wife of twenty-five years.

They chatted but she could see that Nathan was very quiet.

'Do you need the toilet, Nathan?'

'Yes,' was all he said.

Mandy excused them both and said she would show Nathan where the toilet was. As they got downstairs, she ushered him out of the side door and looked at him, just as the rivers of tears started to stream down his face.

'I thought I could do it, but I can't,' he managed between feral sobs.

'Cry it out, Nathan, then suck it up, go back in and see him, tell him you love him and give him a hug. You will never see him again.'

After seeing him today, this much Mandy knew.

Nathan contained himself and went into the bathroom to wash his face. Mandy went back up to the bedroom, Nathan followed and they managed half an hour before the man they loved so much had obviously had enough.

Amy shouted that their sandwiches were ready so they used it as an excuse to leave. More tears from Nathan as they walked downstairs, but he managed to contain it quickly. They settled themselves back into the living room and Amy brought their sandwiches in.

Mandy took a bite out of her sandwich and almost spit it out, but managed to chew it and swallow. She looked at Angel and Nathan and they had the very same reaction. The bacon was hardly cooked, the fat was still on it and virtually raw, this was not going to be pleasant. All Mandy could think was no wonder her dad had lost so much weight.

It brought back a memory, when Dad and Amy had visited in April, Mandy had cooked him his very favourite breakfast, the grill pan. It contained everything he loved; bacon, sausage, black pudding, egg, mushroom, tomatoes and hash browns all grilled together in the grill pan so that he could dip up all of the juices with bread. He had wolfed it down with half a loaf of white bread and told her it had been the best breakfast he had eaten in years. No wonder. Amy had gone mad and told him off, which had made Mandy secretly giggle. All she could think now was what had her dad given up for the sake of a house.

But it was his choice and at least he was being cared for now and Amy did seem to care.

They excused themselves and went upstairs to say goodbye.

As they kissed and hugged, Mandy, whispered, 'I love you, Dad,' in his ear.

He turned, looked her in the eye and said, 'I love you too, you have been my greatest joy, goodbye, Love, my dad is waiting.'

All three of them choked back the tears until they were in the car, then their journey was filled with grief, torrents of tears, talk of the next visit and how bad he looked. Angel was furious about the will being changed, she was his daughter and she had a right yadda, yadda.

'Just stop it, Angel, it is his money and his choice and you need to drop it, your dad is dying, some things are more important.'

Through the talk, Mandy knew that was the last time any of them would see him, and she wanted to crawl into that corner and scream.

Chapter 30
August – Auntie

Wednesday the nineteenth of August and back home with her children, Mandy hugged them both a little harder at every opportunity.

John had been nice when she got back and told him how bad her dad had been, and had told her that she had received a call from Australia from somebody called Hilary.

This was a result; she had been trying to get a hold of her auntie Hilary since her dad's diagnosis using Facebook and last known addresses. Her dad and his sister had fallen out several years ago and they had all lost touch, but Mandy had made it her mission to find her.

Auntie Hilary was the most beautiful, vivacious woman she had ever met and Mandy had adored her as a child. Everybody else had called her vain and selfish, but not to Mandy; to her, she was a goddess and she wanted to be like her.

Dialling the number, she felt hopeful.

'Hello,' the familiar voice said, as sexy as ever.

'Auntie Hilary, it's Mandy, how the hell are you?'

'Oh, darling, it is wonderful to hear from you, I thought we would never speak again due to that silly tantrum from your dad. I think it was the witch he is married to, can't stand the woman, anyway, how are you, my darling?'

'I am fine, but I have some bad news. It's Dad. He has cancer and I don't think he will make it to the end of the month,' Mandy replied sadly.

'Oh no, and I am in Australia and not coming back until mid-September. I am so sorry, darling; you must be devastated.'

'I am heartbroken, but we just have to deal with what is thrown at us, don't we, and it is far worse for Dad than anyone else. We were there yesterday and he looks terrible. I have a feeling that I won't see him again. And I can't stand that woman either,' Mandy gushed.

The conversation went back and forth while they re-acquainted, caught up with each other's lives and put the world to rights. It turned out her auntie Hils had met a man from Liverpool, who lived in Australia, whilst they were both on holiday in Asia, had fallen in love and they were planning to get married so she was spending six months out there to meet his family and friends. You are never too old.

Hilary provided her daughter Caroline's phone number and told Mandy to call her and let her know about her uncle Brian, she was sure that Caroline would want to see him.

They said goodbye and vowed to keep in touch by whatever method was available so that the miles were not a barrier.

Mandy felt a wave of happiness for a few moments. Hearing that beautiful voice and chatting about old times had placed her firmly back into her childhood in Stockport and brought back a tirade of warming and comforting memories. In every memory was her dad cracking terrible jokes, tickling all of the kids and generally being the clown.

Then the happiness melted away and the darkness that is grief gripped her and she sat and sobbed until she couldn't breathe. Why?

Why was he being taken away? He was not old; it just wasn't fair, even though she had been staying positive and mindful about her challenges. The strong one. The one who came up with all of the solutions and practicalities. At this very moment in time, she felt like a little girl who did not know where to turn or what to do and she wanted to give in and give up. The darkness was calling her and it looked inviting. To give up and be with him, to not have to deal with everything, it was tempting. So, tempting.

And as she was being consumed and was wavering something pierced the blackness like a knife. A sound that would wake any mother from the grave. The sound of her child crying.

Jumping up she ran towards the sound and found Dan pinned to the floor by John with Becca screaming and hitting him on the back.

Instinctively she grabbed John, pulled him away and scooped Dan up with her right arm while hugging Becca into her with her left.

'I don't even want to know!' she roared, like the lioness protecting her cubs. 'Get out of my sight.'

96

Without a word, John followed her instructions.

Telling the story through sobs, Becca managed to relay that Dan had been naughty and would not do as her dad had told him so he had gone to smack him and Dan had run away. John had chased him through the house, jumped on him and pinned him down. Becca was brave and had tried to save her little brother but John's rage had been too scary.

'Well, I really do think you are the bravest girl I have ever met, Becca, trying to save your brother. You are my hero.'

'And mine,' Dan piped up.

There it was. The reason that she could not let the darkness take over. A timely reminder of the challenges she was facing and why she had to win. There was no loss in this game, win or die and she was not going to die.

Chapter 31
August – Positivity

Having dealt with John upon his return the previous evening and threatening him within an inch of his life, Mandy had certainty ensured that there would be no similar incidents with his temper in the short time he had left in this house.

Calling Cousin Caroline had been emotional, they had both cried. They had then proceeded to have almost the same catch up as the previous day with Auntie Hilary. This time though there was no darkness, just the positive mindset that Mandy had decided would never leave her again. Caroline had been so sad about her uncle; she wanted to come and see him.'

'Well, we will be visiting next Tuesday the twenty-fifth if you want to come with us?' Mandy assured Caroline.

'That would be ace, cous. I know that things haven't been great for the last few years, but I still love my uncle Brian and would love to see him before it's too late,' Caroline responded, with a sadness in her voice that was tangible.

'I will sort arrangements out with Angel and let you know, maybe we could meet somewhere and go in together, I'll call you on Monday.'

'Fab, Mand, speak then.' She hung up and left Mandy feeling happier for re-connecting with family before it was too late for her dad.

Beach trips, long dog walks and lots of ice cream were the plans for the next few days. School holidays had always been elusive, something that slipped by with John seeming to have all of the fun while she was at work. It turns out that had been the biggest lie of all because Becca had told her that they never left the front garden with their dad. He just wanted to play computer games. She thanked the universe that she had filled the front garden with everything a child could wish for, a swing set, slide, trampoline, bikes, sandpit, you name it, her kids had it, even a mini bouncy castle. However, they would always rather be splodging in rock pools for crabs, building sandcastles, moats and swimming in the sea with the dogs.

They would be outside at every opportunity for this final couple of weeks of the holidays. Their summer holiday had been stolen by cancer. Their precious time with their happy mum had been put on hold by cancer and secret challenges. So, Mandy had decided to just have a few days of fun.

Since her little blip and facing the darkness after she had spoken to her auntie Hilary, she had managed to maintain an intensely positive mindset. Organising every little detail of everything, she had created action plans; written some great content and learnings in her book; thought about the future as a single mum and the dreaded court proceedings she would have to attend for the bankruptcy.

She had thought about trying to stash some of her money away prior to the court hearing but did not want to end up in prison for fraud so she was going to follow the rules. There had been enough illegal and immoral activity around her from her supposed loved ones, so she felt the need to be authentic and honest.

Whatever challenges remained to test her; she would face them directly with a solution-based approach. Having reflected long and hard on her moment of weakness, she had surmised that it was just human to feel like that and that she was no different from the next person in her responses. What made her different was her ability to not let the negativity take her down. Not everyone had that ability, it was a special skill. This was going to be the skill that helped her to win.

When she thought about where this skill had developed from, she smiled.

'You are the best girl in the world and you can do anything you put your mind to. If anyone ever tells you otherwise, take no notice of them because they don't see what I see,' her dad would tell her at every opportunity.

She believed him because he was her hero and wouldn't lie. What a gift he had given her. The gift of self-belief.

It was this strong self-belief that had enabled her to go for it in school, at work and in life, never letting anything stop her or alter her path. She had known what she wanted, gone out to get it and been successful. Studying hard, working hard, standing her ground and fighting for those who could not fight for themselves, she had created a reputation of integrity and inspiration. Never taking no for an answer, she had forged her way to the top in record time, in the right way by empowering and leading others. People had wanted to be around her and learn from her.

Now, more than ever, she needed to utilise those skills and hone them to serve her ongoing. As sure as she ever had been that she could win, she had re-instated her positive mindset and self-belief and was ready for anything.

Just then John walked in the room.

'Look,' she said, 'we can be civil but we are not being authentic. I want to tell the kids, there is no point in putting it off, and I want you to tell them that it is because you don't love me and you have found someone else. You owe me that.'

John was taken aback, but sat down and agreed to tell the kids the next day.

'What about me moving out?' he asked.

'I think it would be sensible for you to be looking into this now with a view that you will be out in a few weeks. In the meantime, we need to be prepared for lots of questions from Becca and some tears. We need to deal with this positively and consistently. OK?'

John agreed, but Mandy was unsure if his priorities included anybody other than himself. By expecting the worst from him, maybe it wouldn't be that difficult to deal with this when it showed up.

Chapter 32
August – Honesty

The bright sunshine lit up the front room and warmed the very bones of you. The sofa was hot, the carpet was warm and cosy beneath bare feet and it seemed as good and as positive a time as any for Mandy and John to reveal what was happening to their children.

Her heart was beating hard and fast, her breaths were short and sharp. Never before had she felt as nervous and apprehensive, not even prior to the most important meetings or hugely important speaking events, this was way worse.

She had carried on with the usual morning routine, walked the dogs, made pancakes with her helpers and tried to act as normal as possible. But, her very astute nine-year-old who was wise beyond her years was already asking questions.

'Mum, are you OK?'

'What makes you ask that, Becca?' was her tepid response.

'You don't feel like mum today,' Becca replied.

'Well, I can assure you, I most definitely still am your mum, now give me ten minutes then you and Dan come down and we can decide where we are going today.'

Mandy had already prepared herself for what might happen and made the decision to take the kids out somewhere on her own so they could ask questions.

'OK, Mum,' Becca said skipping upstairs.

Trying to keep her anger at John under control for forcing her to hurt her children was difficult, and it was entwined with feelings of relief and optimism that in turn manifested as guilt. Mum guilt, it showed up in every single decision that you made in life, from how to punish them, going out for a night to going to work. It was like tendrils pulling you so far down from the person you were so that you felt you would never meet them again in your lifetime. Then on the flip side was the joy and love that was experienced every time you so much as glanced at your child and that pulled you back up and erased that guilt and kept you moving forward. This was the right thing to do for the long game.

Sitting in the living room waiting for the kids to come in for what seemed like an eternity, John was there but there was no conversation. Just the sounds of the cows on the farm and the occasional tractor passing by. Eventually, and with too much relief, Mandy heard two sets of little footsteps pattering down the stairs and coming towards them. Bracing herself and willing her eyes to stay dry, she was ready.

'Where are we going then?' Becca exclaimed as she burst into the room with her usual energy and enthusiasm.

'Just sit down the both of you, we have something we want to tell you.' Mandy replied, trying hard to disguise the hurt that pierced her heart because of what she was about to do.

'Are we getting a new brother or sister, because you have been acting weird, Mum?' was Becca's innocent response.

It almost made Mandy laugh out loud because it was so far from the awful truth that she was about to deliver to her precious babies.

'No, but I am going to let your dad tell you,' she replied, looking at John as his prompt to commence proceedings.

He coughed and looked uncomfortable, but sat forward and started to speak.

'Well, you two, I am really sorry, but I just don't love your mum anymore and I have met someone else, so, unfortunately, we will be getting a divorce,' he managed to blurt out, rather abruptly and with no added embellishments, but he had done what he promised.

Becca stared. Dan looked like what had just been said had floated over his head.

'Look, guys, this just happens sometimes when mum's and dad's no longer get along, and it is better that you know what is coming. Your dad will be going in a few weeks as soon as he has found somewhere to live. Dan, you can move into Mum's room and your dad can have your room, if that is OK with you?' Mandy offered.

Dan was instantly interested in the prospect of sleeping with his mum and watching the big telly in the big bed. Becca, however, was planning her response carefully and Mandy could almost see it ticking over in her head.

'So, who will we live with?' was her first question.

'With me, sweetie, but you can see your dad as often as you like.'

'Will the dogs be with us?' was the second question.

'Yes, they will, it will be me, you guys and the dogs,' Mandy responded as positively as she could manage.

'Well, that's OK then, I am not bothered about seeing him, now when are we going?'

She nodded towards her dad then looked directly at Mandy with a get me out of here as quickly as possible look.

'Go and get your shoes on, anything you want to take and the dogs lead's and we will go in a minute,' was Mandy's slightly stunned reply.

And off they both ran; as simple as that. As if nothing had happened.

Mandy looked at John and said, 'I will talk to them while I am out.'

To which he replied, 'To be honest, I am just glad it's over and if she doesn't want to see me then that's fine.'

'She is only nine, John, and probably shocked and upset.'

'She's like her bloody mother more like, only interested in herself; well, see if I care, I can't wait to get away from the lot of you. Your bloody family, your friends all of it, especially your lunatic sister. I am sick of you being Mrs fucking perfect, I am sick of your sister always needing money, I am sick of all your friends who look down on me, it's all fucked up.'

He stormed out of the living room almost knocking Becca over as she was heading back in, and in that one paragraph outburst he had summed it up. He was jealous, he felt not worthy and he blamed it all on Mandy.

'Poor me syndrome,' she said out loud.

'What does that mean, Mum?' Becca asked as she came through the door.

'It means someone who blames their own failings on everyone else and then seeks sympathy from others.' She just decided to tell Becca as there was no point in lying anymore.

'That would be Dad then,' Becca replied matter-of-factly.

Why was her little girl so amazing? John had been right there as well; she was just like her mother.

They set off for another beach day and Mandy promised fish and chips, ice creams and a treat each from the shops at Sea houses. They both asked questions in the car but Mandy could only describe them as practical questions. Neither of them seemed surprised, upset or at all phased at the prospects of John not being there; in fact, if anything, they seemed happy. She wondered why but was not going to ask that question today, the answer would no doubt unveil itself in the future, when they were ready.

What they did do that day was have fun, she knew that her children would remember this day for a long time, if not for the rest of their lives, so she wanted to attach happiness to the memories, so that is exactly what she did.

Chapter 33
August – Final

The weekend had passed over without any tears or tantrums and Mandy had been amazed at her children. They had asked some questions which she had answered honestly. John had dipped in and out infrequently and seemed sorry for what he had said and had tried to interact with them to the best of his capabilities.

She pondered and came to the conclusion that he did actually love his kids, but he just didn't want to be a dad. He had made that clear when she fell pregnant with Dan. But she still didn't think he was a really horrible person, although this would change in the coming months; right now, she settled herself with this perception because it enabled her to be civil and fair in their dealings.

Tomorrow was Tuesday the twenty-fifth of August and there was only a week of the school holidays left, the kids went back to school next Wednesday the second of September. Mandy had arranged to meet her cousin Caroline at the services just outside Manchester before heading to see her dad. He had been taken back into hospital because Amy could not cope with him, despite his wish to die at home. So, they were going to set off for the hospital from the services. She was picking Angel up at the usual time. She was really dreading this visit but knew she had to go as it may be the last chance to see her dad alive. Every time she thought about his death, it hit her like a tidal wave, the grief, the void it would leave in her heart and she could hardly bear it.

But, like the trooper she was, she shook it off and kept going for everyone else, but mostly for herself. As she was in that thought, her mobile rang, it was Amy, reluctantly she picked it up.

'Hi, Amy, how are you?' she asked politely.

'I'm fine, glad to have some time to get my hair done, I feel like I have let myself go with all of this business. Anyway, your dad doesn't want any visitors tomorrow.'

Stunned at the context of that sentence, Mandy searched for the right words.

'OK, well I am sorry he feels that way, but both you and I know that this may be our last chance to see him and even if I get five minutes, I am coming,' was her thoughtful reply.

'Well, he wants nothing to do with the offspring of his awful sister, so you had better re-think that.'

And with that, she hung up.

Mandy knew that this woman was manipulative and that she made her dad think the same as she did, but this was beyond belief. Caroline was his niece and had done no harm to either of them. It was like this woman had spent the last thirteen years that they had been together trying to turn him against everyone. She was bitter, she was sickly sweet and pathetically presented so that she could be seen as everybody's friend when in fact she was a silent ninja filled with hate. At this point, when the man was dying, why not let him see people who loved him? She had tried to keep him to herself in life and now it was like she wanted every piece of the last moments of it as well, controlling his death like she controlled his life.

He was managed in detail by this woman. She bought his clothes, laid them out for him, told him what to eat, how to behave and now she was telling him how to die.

'Not on my bloody watch,' she said out loud. 'We are coming and meeting Caroline and she is coming, he will love seeing her.'

It was like she was convincing herself by speaking out loud, but she wasn't convinced. Amy had won in life with all but her, she could not make him hate her, but she would now go out of her way for a win here, Mandy knew it.

Mandy also knew she was under observation and had to make the right decisions, but what was right?

'Give me a sign grandad!' she asked while looking upwards.

But no sign came. There were no signs, no help, nobody else that could know, just herself, her decisions and her hope that each one was the right one.

She would do what she had planned and trust her gut.

Her sleep that night was filled with vivid dreams of death. Her death, her dad's death and both the desire to go with him and the need to stay. She woke exhausted but ready to see him once more, so she set off promptly to collect her sister and headed down the long road from Northumberland to Manchester for the penultimate time.

They arrived at the services early to meet Caroline, and there was this stunningly beautiful woman, just like Auntie Hilary, who was so warm and down to earth. Who wouldn't love her? They had coffee and a bite to eat and caught up.

'I spoke to Amy and she told me he didn't want any visitor's today but I insisted that we go,' Mandy told Caroline.

'Fuck her, I say,' Angel chipped in.

'Do you think I should go, our Mand?' asked Caroline.

'Until instructed otherwise, then yes, I actually think he would love to see you, but Amy is most definitely in control here,' she responded feeling sad.

'Fucking cow,' Angel chipped in again.

'If you can't say anything positive, keep it zipped, Angel, now is not a time for more hate, there is enough of that floating around,' Mandy chastised.

'Well, I'm entitled to my opinion,' she replied.

'Of course, just keep it to yourself, our main concern is Dad.'

They set off from the services and made their way to the hospital. Just five minutes from the hospital the phone rang and Angel answered. It was Amy, as expected, and she was adamant that Caroline was not welcome, but they were granted their five minutes. Angel called Caroline and told her, she was upset but understood and Mandy said she would call her when she got home tonight.

When they arrived at the hospital Amy was there, like a guard on the door with perfect hair, eyebrows and makeup. They were given instructions and told to only stay the five minutes.

As they entered the ward he was sleeping, so they each pulled up a chair and Mandy gently touched his arm. His eyes flickered and he was with them. He was thin and weak but the biggest smile came over his face.

'Girls,' he said.

And Mandy knew he had not asked for anything, he could hardly speak.

'Hi, Dad,' she replied. 'How are you holding up?'

It was a pretty stupid question, but all that she could think to say.

'I am ready. I have spoken to George and he is coming. Me for you, and I am ready for a rest,' was his wobbly response.

George was his dad, her grandad, the man who had met her and negotiated her deal. She felt a wave of peace come over her. Maybe she had misheard him because it was more of a whisper but she thought he had said George was coming for me and you, that can't be what he said?

They managed a few words and stayed exactly eleven minutes, refusing to stick to their imposed curfew. Amy gave them a death stare when they came out of the ward, why would she begrudge them this piece of time? She would never understand, but she was polite as usual as they left.

Both of them sat in the car and wept, there was no being strong after that visit. They had spoken their last words with their beloved dad, were forced to leave and have no more interaction in the time he had left. That was hard to take.

It was a sombre drive home. Mandy called Caroline and told her what had happened, and she was amazing.

'He is on morphine and in and out of sleep, so I am sure he is in no pain.'

'Well, that is a Godsend, cous, keep me informed and I would really like to come to the funeral,' Caroline had said.

'Oh, you are coming, we will stand together and say goodbye.'

With that call over, sheer exhaustion hit her like a high-speed train and she slept like she had not been able to in weeks, knowing that she had done all that she could do and said goodbye to the best man that she had ever had the good fortune to know.

Chapter 34
First of September
2009 – Goodbye

It was the first of September and it had been a week of focusing on the kids, buying new uniforms, trips out and daily updates from Amy.

It was 11 a.m. when the call came. Amy's number came up on the ID and Mandy pressed the answer button already knowing.

'Your dad died this morning peacefully in his sleep,' Amy said through tears.

'Were you there?' was all Mandy could think of to say.

'No, I was having my nails done, but the nurse was with him and he just took one deep breath and he was gone, she said it was so peaceful, they have been amazing the nurses. Anyway, we have to wait for an autopsy and I will keep you informed, will you let everybody know.'

It was almost a matter of fact.

'I will, thanks,' Mandy replied and hung up.

She wanted to scream. Her dad had died alone while his wife was getting her nails done and they were not allowed any more than five minutes. She would have camped by his bed, what was going on? She could not make sense of it. Oh my God, she wanted to scream, but there were no tears. Anger and disgust took over. Her beautiful, amazing dad died alone. Not surrounded by people who love him like in the movies. Alone. This was a bitter blow and was really going to test her patience, her control and her behaviour. She knew it wouldn't change anything no matter what she did, but this was more than a challenge.

She dutifully called everyone except Angel, then jumped in the car and drove to the pub. When she walked in Angel took one look at her and just collapsed in tears. They had all known, all been waiting but it still does not make it any easier when it happens. She stayed for about an hour to console her sister then went home to tell the kids who were out for ice cream with Nana.

They weren't home when she arrived so she wrote down the details in her diary and took the dogs out for a long walk to clear her mind. This would be a day she would remember every second of for the rest of her life. She was hurting, that painful hurt like when you broke up with your first love and you feel like you will never get over it, but she knew that now, more than ever, she needed to think straight. She spoke to her dad on the dog walk and told him that she would see him again and that she hoped that he felt himself again. The main focus was readying herself to tell the kids that their grandad had died. Dan would not even remember him in a few years and was too young to really understand, Becca always would and would be devastated.

At home, John was there so she told him and he had cried, her dad was easy to love. Her mum arrived back with the kids and she told her and she cried, they had been married for twenty-five years after all. So, to the job of telling the kids, Dan didn't know what to say but Becca was heartbroken and inconsolable. For the rest of that day, she would be constantly bursting into tears and saying that she missed her grandad while Dan would simply ask where he was living now.

These two beautiful children had kept her going through every challenge so far and would keep doing so. They were her inspiration, her reason for wanting to stay and always would be. Like everything else that had happened so far, she would face this challenge with strength and courage for their sake.

1.9.09 RIP Brian King.

110

Chapter 35
September – Life

Life goes on, so they say. And it does, the same old things have to be done. However, this was not the same old for Mandy, because having just faced the toughest challenge so far, she could not help but hope for that to be the end with no more to come. She needed time. But that would not be the way it turned out.

The autopsy had revealed that the cancer was everywhere but had started in his spine. Mandy thought that breaking his neck when he was young had been the cause, but she would never receive an answer to that question.

John had been looking for somewhere to live but was not having much luck and his mother was not happy for him to move in with her because she would lose her benefits. She had been on the phone every other day complaining, completely oblivious that Mandy really did not want to hear because she had just lost her dad. Mandy now knew exactly where John's "poor me" syndrome had come from. Things were getting difficult with John still being there so the quicker the better as far as she was concerned, however, she was also more than aware that this could be another challenge and she would just have to get on with it like it or not.

The funeral was scheduled for the ninth of September. 9/11, a day when so many had lost their lives in a needless way, would also be the day she said her final goodbye to her dad.

Pleading with Amy to let her read a eulogy had been exhausting but she had eventually dropped it for her allowing Caroline to attend the funeral. Not to be beaten, Mandy had arranged to read the eulogy in the car park of the crematorium after the funeral to the nine members of her family who were attending. Auntie Hilary had been heartbroken at not being able to attend and say her goodbye's, but that was the way things were turning out.

On the day of the funeral, there were two cars full from Northumberland and Caroline was meeting them there. They had arrived at the house as arranged prior to the funeral and Mandy and Angel had decided to go to the funeral home to view the body in the casket. Amy had tried to come with them but Mandy had put her foot down insisting that they wanted to say their own goodbye, she had her opportunity and now it was theirs. Taken aback but allowing this one Amy had agreed.

When they arrived and were taken through, they were both a bit overwhelmed having never done this before. He looked so peaceful but Amy had him dressed in a baby blue silk collar which he would have hated. Mandy had written a letter and sneaked it in the coffin with him but managed to keep her composure. Angel, however, was a wreck again. It was a moment that they would remember for the rest of their lives.

Goodbyes were hard. This goodbye was extremely hard, but to remain composed was her aim and stick to it she absolutely would.

They headed back to the house where the cars would leave from in about half an hour. They had been allowed into the main car with Amy, it would have been a talking point had they not been. Mingling back at the house with all of Amy's friends was hard work, everyone was saying sorry and Amy was periodically wailing and attracting sympathy. It was when the funeral car with the coffin rolled up and Amy threw herself to the floor screaming, "Nooooooo, Brian," in a very dramatic soap opera fashion that Mandy felt she definitely had the strength to get through the day. Exiting when this happened to join her family who were all standing there snickering, lightened the mood completely. Her dad would have pissed himself laughing at that display. So, while all of her friends gathered around her offering sympathy in buckets, the real King family had a giggle at the back door. *Thanks, Dad,* she thought.

When the time came to leave, another soap opera display from the weeping widow and more giggles from the King's. This was going to be such a help; she knew her dad was there helping every step of the way.

On arrival at the crematorium, the King family were seated way back with the exception of Mandy and Angel who were allowed in the front row with Amy. Gritting teeth throughout the service which was delivered by a vicar who did not even know her dad; in a very generic way, they could not wait to leave. It was impersonal, excluded his sister, nephew and niece in the mention of family members which stood out as the moment that Mandy ultimately decided that she would never see Amy again after today. After the service had finished, they filtered out into the car park and did not stay to shake hands with all of the attendees that they did not know.

Reading the eulogy, she had written with love, in the car park with her family there was the most emotional moment of the day. They went to the wake for a courteous amount of time and witnessed the weeping widow once again in between her laughing and joking with her friends. She was highly manicured, bouffant haired, spray-tanned and eyebrows tattooed in place and not a person that any of them wished to set eyes on again as long as they lived. Driving away that day felt good in one way and so sad in another. But Mandy knew she did not need Manchester, nor a grave to know that her dad was with her, he would always be with her.

When they arrived home that night, she was completely exhausted. Dan and the dogs had missed her and were all over her like a rash. Once everyone was in bed, she sat down to finish her diary. The eulogy would be the last entry.

It was a short book because of the forty-three days from diagnoses to death, but it was powerful and raw. She would send it to the publisher next week in honour of a great man. Her good friend and artist, another Mandy, had finished the illustrations, so it was ready to go.

When she wearily slid into bed sleep would come quickly and be deep and undisturbed. Her dreams were filled with memories and love and she was sure she had seen her dad and grandad sitting at the end of her bed but didn't remember this waking up so she put it down to being just a dream.

The next day saw a normal routine return and the practicalities of day-to-day life. She found unpaid bills because everything was still her responsibility and she had been distracted. Then there was the court date for the bankruptcy hearing, which was on her birthday at the beginning of October. Once she had done the school run, she paid the bills and scheduled her diary with the appointments that she had received letters for. Angel phoned to say she had received her eviction date and could now go to the council for a house. She was thinking about moving further away now because she was ashamed and felt suicidal again because of the pub and the debt. Mandy listened but felt too exhausted to offer any help or solutions. She just wanted to get her own house in order with being a single parent being imminent. This was not what Angel wanted to hear and she hung up the phone. We all grieve in our own way.

Chapter 36
September – Calm

All Mandy wanted now was a period of calm to be able to grieve, but the universe seemed to have a different idea. John was under her feet with no sign of moving. She had some part-time work cleaning, so she had gone from being a senior leader to a cleaner. She could claim some lone parent support once John left but nothing until then which was frustrating and in just over three weeks, she had to attend the bankruptcy hearing and would have to surrender all of her remaining money. To top that Angel was really angry again, obviously her way of lashing out but there didn't seem to be any way of consoling her. She decided to deal with the biggest issue first and called John's mother to see if she could convince her to take him in.

'Look, Elsie, I know this is a problem for you, but it is confusing and upsetting for the kids and I think we need to have a clean break. I have seen a solicitor about divorce and there is no going back. He needs to move out soon,' Mandy pleaded.

'Well, I am just worried about my benefits, I will lose about thirty pounds a week, you know.'

'So, make him get a job and pay you board, it's simple,' Mandy responded.

'Well, it's not that easy for him you know, there are not as many jobs over here. Let me think about it and I will let you know,' Elsie replied.

'Well, make it quick because I will be packing his stuff and leaving it in the cow sheds if he isn't out in a week,' she said in the hopes that it would make a difference and ended the call.

'I hope that is enough,' she said to herself.

John was the "golden boy" and his mother made allowances for every failure and cock up in his life. She had even known about the affair and never uttered a word supporting him instead because Mandy was difficult to live with. The fact that John had been a kept man, enjoyed beautiful homes, holidays abroad, a luxury lifestyle and never had to work was never acknowledged. If he was unhappy then it was as much his fault as hers but that would be bypassed in any conversations. Poor John, he has had a hell of a life! She could almost hear what was being said about her, but she let it wash over her with dignity and put her children first and foremost in her decision making.

That is exactly what she had pledged to do now for the rest of her life. This state of adversity she found herself in was temporary because she knew that she was graced with natural leadership and entrepreneurial talent which would show her the way back out. The revelations in the study of "The Secret" and all of its component parts, the advanced diplomas in coaching she had achieved and the academic qualifications she already had would be her knowledge foundations. She would continue to read and study once she had settled as a single, bankrupt mum with a cleaning job and she would rise again. This time it would be higher, she would exceed even her own expectations because that is how high she was prepared to set her goals.

She had no clue yet exactly what this new success looked like, sounded like or felt like, but she was prepared to overcome every obstacle, smash down every comfort zone and just go for it. This mindset was being born from her understanding that when you hit rock bottom, and she felt she was well on her way there, that there really is only one place that you can go. Choice, it is all about choice and she was going to choose success and trust that the powers would light the way once she had completed all of her challenges. This trust in the universe and life had crept into her very soul, unnoticed, like a silent angel and she had welcomed it. Fear would no longer be a welcome at her table, only hope, optimism and the lessons she had learned in her life were sitting there and they were welcome to drink from her chalice.

She felt calm, positive, focused and well. The feeling was good, even though her heart was still aching for her dad, she knew in her bones that she would see him again and that he was present right now soothing and sharing his love for her. He had always been her biggest fan, encouraging, nurturing and challenging her to be the best version of herself, she would not let him, nor herself down now.

'A little help in encouraging John to move quickly would be good, Dad,' she uttered out loud and smiled because she knew he was listening.

Life did settle into some sort of weird routine that involved absolutely everything being her responsibility and John lying in bed until lunchtime then going to his part-time job, which he kept all of his earnings from, then heading off out to be with his new girlfriend. No amount of encouragement with his mother seemed to be moving her from her negative position, but Mandy kept chipping away.

The bankruptcy hearing date was looming in the next week and Mandy was readying herself for how she might feel. Trying to remain positive but feeling shame and dread.

Having never been out of control with her finances, this was something she had never expected and the feelings associated with the event that lay ahead were new and unnatural. Angel, however, had experienced mismanagement of her personal finances, debtors and difficulty but was proving to be out of control in her behaviour and her approach, which was actually no help to Mandy at all.

Chapter 37
October – Angel

It was eventually October and there were two monumental events that Mandy knew she, firstly, could not avoid, and secondly did not want to be sucked into.

The bankruptcy hearing was to be at Newcastle Court on the third of October, the day after her birthday, happy bloody birthday. But more daunting than that was Angel's eviction date from the pub on the seventeenth of October. The Brewery had been lenient with time but were now pressing for her to be out. Angel was spiralling and lashing out, so Mandy had made the brave decision to enter the lion's den and just face the inevitable backlash. She was on her way to the pub.

'Is anybody here?' she shouted with eyes closed and awaiting the explosion.

'What the fuck do you want?' was the not so welcome response from her sister.

'I am just worried and wanted to come and see how you are doing, how you are feeling and what your plans are, that's all,' Mandy offered in the hopes of peace.

'Have them bastards at the brewery sent you to harass me?' was the bitter retort.

'Not at all, I am your sister and I am allowed to actually care about you,' Mandy offered softly and with genuine empathy.

'Why the fuck would YOU care about a fat useless fuck like me?' Angel replied, her voice starting to break and the tears in her eyes were magnified by her glasses.

Mandy's heart broke. Even though her sister was useless with money, she loved her. No matter how many times she had failed, cocked up, made epic mistakes, she loved her, and she felt a strong sense of responsibility for her.

Whatever anybody else thought, Angel had not had it easy. They had amazing parents, but they had split up when Angel was still at home, however, Mandy was independent and living away, so that had been hard on her sister. Angel had been bullied her entire life about her weight, and to add to that she had suffered from acne and the scars from it on her face, had sight problems and always needed glasses, so she had been a target for other children. Even though Mandy had also had the same weight issues, she had taken control of it a few times, although right now she was bigger than ever having used her "go-to" comfort to get through her unhappy marriage. The difference was that Mandy did not let her size define her, she knew she was worthy no matter what she looked like outwardly, whereas her sister had a deep-rooted hatred for herself that seemed to drive everything she did and every choice she made.

An addictive personality does not only show up with alcohol and drugs. Angel had been a food addict her entire life, and with a mother who was a "post-war" feeder, that habit had grown to immense proportions. Having tried to take her own life with her mother's diazepam at eleven years old, Angel had been wrapped in cotton wool by all of them in compensation and given everything she had demanded. She had demanded a lot. Food, alcohol, cigarettes had all been Angel's vices, with not one of them seeming to ease the torment that was taking place inside of her. Choosing to be the clown so that she didn't have to deal with these demons and become a responsible adult, Angel had eventually found her fourth vice, spending money she did not have. The constant debt, followed by alcohol abuse and binge eating accompanied with a minimum of a twenty a day tobacco habit, happened cyclically.

It went, buy nice things for instant gratification, by any means possible, be it credit cards, catalogues or loans. Don't pay it back and get depressed when creditors came knocking and turn to booze and food. Await the cavalry following the "I want to die" threats, then do it all again once the debts were settled.

Every time felt like Groundhog Day. But as enablers, Mandy, her mum and dad would dutifully fulfil their roles. Until Dad said no more. Then Angel blamed Amy and vowed never to speak to him again. Until he was diagnosed with cancer then she had guilt, which made her hate herself, and by the way, she was in monumental debt again and here we were doing the same old dance.

Snapped back to the present by weeping, Mandy went over to her sister and gently put her arm around Angel's shoulders and said, 'Look, Sis, no matter how bad things look, there is always something you can do, you know.'

118

'That is easy for you, you seem to cope with anything. I am so shit at everything. I can't get over losing Dad, I am ashamed about this bankruptcy shit and I just keep getting pissed and eating junk food. I have found a house in Whitby but I can't afford the deposit and bond. Mum says she will try and help as a guarantor but we just can't get the money. I need to get away from everything and everybody and start fresh.'

Mandy couldn't stop the words coming out of her mouth, despite her head screaming, 'NO, how much do you need?'

'Including removals, twelve hundred pounds,' Angel replied, instantly stopping crying, they had been here before and it had always ended the same.

'I will give it to you if you promise me that you will try and get some help when you get down there. It will be the very last time I will be able to help because I am about to lose everything, so NEVER ask me again, do you hear?'

It was said with regret and a heavy heart because she knew she shouldn't be doing it, but she also knew she had to let her sister go if she was ever going to stand a chance of getting her own life back on track. Whitby was far enough away to be able to do that.

'I promise,' Angel said.

But she had said that a million times before as well, this time, however, was the last time because Mandy had already made the decision that she would never help her sister again. If this was the challenge then she would make sure she stuck to it, not only for the test but for her own sanity and survival.

'Right then, Angel, get yourself sorted and removals booked and I will pick you up for the bankruptcy hearing next week. I will transfer the money to you when I get home, OK.'

'Thanks, I will try,' replied Angel, but Mandy knew that she didn't mean it.

Not because she didn't want to but because Angel's demons were fiercer than ever, almost visible and they would win again. This meant that her sister was in for a very rough ride, on her own, and although that broke Mandy's heart, it also enabled her to feel a little lighter and see a little clearer.

Chapter 38
October – Shame

It was the day of the bankruptcy hearing and Mandy was feeling sick to the stomach. Having only ever entered a courtroom to obtain her alcohol license for her retail roles and the pub, or to give evidence against shoplifters, it was a whole different ball game being the accused. She felt embarrassed and a huge amount of shame. Not because of the debt itself, but because she had constantly made such poor decisions when it came to her sister and men.

She wondered why she was so good at identifying and developing talent in the workplace, somewhere where her success had been so great because of her team selection and growth, and yet she was so poor at selecting the traits necessary to make a good partner. Perhaps, the co-dependent relationship with her sister played a part in blurring what a good relationship or partner looked like. Having studied so hard and read so many books since the car accident, which felt like an age ago, but was only a few months, she could acknowledge that her recognition of her role in relationships was more informed. What was beginning to become clear was that she really needed some time on her own and away from her sister to enable her to decide what it was that would make her happy and fulfilled, even if that answer was not what she wanted to hear.

Today would see her make a final break with her sister, no matter how shameful the context was. John was still in and out of the house like a ghost, taking on none of his parental responsibilities but refusing to leave any time soon. The kids were confused but happy and Mandy was making their new normal as easy as she possibly could. Today would be a line in the sand for many things, and people, and almost like a starting line for her new beginning. She would be debt-free, but unable to obtain credit for six years. New learnings were heading her way at full speed. No savings, no backup plans, no rainy day or holiday funds, just survival. She was ready.

Pulling up outside the pub for the last time she tooted the horn and waited. Angel arrived after a few minutes, and huffed into the passenger seat, reeking of alcohol and cigarettes.

'Let's get this the fuck over with then,' was her welcome. No morning, sis, thanks for your help, nice to see you, just the comment of a disturbed woman with no self-esteem who was about to have it hammered down one more peg.

The drive was quiet, with Angel falling asleep a couple of times and offering little in the way of conversation when she was awake and lucid. Parking was a challenge when they arrived and they were running late, which is something Mandy did not do well. This resulted in her feeling stressed and not her usual cool self, or maybe that was the fact that this whole situation could have been avoided if she had just said no to her sister. She was angry and feeling like blaming everyone else for her situation.

Blame was a dark subject to her. Having lived with a man who could take no responsibility for any of his actions and had a lifetime with her sister who blamed everything on anybody but herself, all of a sudden, like the ceiling had lifted from the courtroom, she experienced an epiphany.

Stopping in her tracks, on the stairs, she blurted, 'I am responsible!'

Angel's head swung around and she looked a bit stunned.

'For what?'

'I am responsible for everything,' Mandy replied.

Angel looked at her like she had grown a second head and said, 'We are going to be late.'

So, off they ran and made it just in time. But Mandy no longer cared about what was about to happen. The act of taking on the responsibility for everything and accepting that it was all her choice and her doing had created a pathway that was not there earlier. It was like her mind had shifted and so had her heart. She was really ready to take this on the chin and move on, so she entered the courtroom with her head high and left the same way.

Dropping Angel back at the pub, they said their goodbyes and Mandy headed home feeling relieved. The debt was gone and Angel would soon be gone. Now to the task of removing the final negative force that was holding her back. She was prepared to deal with this head-on now and force John's hand no matter what the consequences were. She had done her time and had enough.

Chapter 39
October – John

The day after the bankruptcy hearing was D-Day as far as Mandy was concerned. John was still in bed and she was bracing herself for a battle that she was determined to win. Lying awake all night she had rehearsed what she was going to say and how she was going to say it. John would be defensive, difficult and aggressive, but she would be bullied no more. The plan was to lay the cards on the table and tell him what was going to happen with no wriggle room. It was her time to remove this thorn from her side and allow herself and her children to establish their new reality. He would be an obstacle no more.

Knocking firmly on the bedroom door she assertively announced, 'John, get up please, we need to talk.'

Mumbles from the other side of the door to say he would be down in ten and could she make him a coffee.

'You can make your own coffee when you get downstairs, I don't have all day, so hurry up.'

That felt good.

Eventually, looking dishevelled, to say the least with greasy hair and at least three days' beard growth, John appeared looking decidedly sheepish.

'I can't be arsed with an argument with your mind, you are always fucking right anyway, so what is it? Just get it over with,' was his greeting.

'Delightful as ever,' she said but carried on, 'I am fed up with the situation here. I want you gone. The kids are confused, neither of us can move on with our lives and I don't think you will ever go if I don't force your hand. I am giving you until the end of October to pack your stuff up and move out. If you have nowhere to go, I suggest you go and have a long conversation with your mother and your girlfriend. This is not up for negotiation by the way. If you are not gone by the thirty first of October, your things will be found lying next to the cowshed on the first of November, is that clear enough for you?'

There was a resolution in her voice that obviously made an impact on the Neanderthal standing in front of her.

'I will do my best,' was all he could manage.

'That is not good enough, your best is regularly poor, this is non-negotiable, let me make that perfectly clear. I am now bankrupt; you are not contributing to this home and yet you are living here. The only people you are hurting are your children, so if there is an ounce of decency left in you, you will make sure you are gone.'

This was a clear ultimatum on her part and she was not budging in the slightest.

'OK, OK, I will be gone.'

'Good, now try and avoid me for the remainder of the time you are here, please.'

And with that, she walked away having made her point loud and clear.

Deciding to go out with the dogs and have a nice long walk to get out of his way until he left for work, she felt good. The boys were their usual boisterous selves, excited for walkies.

She loved living here in the middle of the stunning Northumbrian countryside, so far from civilisation but still so near. They had seen this place to rent when they had first moved back up north, choosing the rental market instead of buying so as not to tie up all of their savings. It was a retreat that could have been at home in a Dickensian novel. A drive down a bumpy country road, really made for a coach and horses, past the Manor House and around a corner to two old farmhouse cottages adjacent to the byre. Views to die for from every angle and a private farm road that took them on a walk they referred to as the "triangle" as that is how it was laid out around the properties. Many an activity had taken place around "the triangle". Becca had learned her multiplication tables one at a time walking around it; they had been blackberry picking every year around it; they had trained the dogs around it and Mandy had even taught Nathan how to drive around it. It was the best triangle that Mandy could think of.

The house itself was a massive old farmhouse converted into two dwellings. With thick stone walls, sash windows, oil central heating and a coal fire, it was home. The rooms were spacious with high ceilings and there was so much storage space. The smell from the byre was a bit overpowering at times, but it was offset by all of the positives. The children could play safely outside and in winter, they built snowmen and curled up in front of the coal fire and made toast.

As she walked, dogs barking and playing at her side, she thought about her realisation at the court. Accepting full responsibility for her current situation, acknowledging that all of the decisions she had made were the best ones she knew how to make at the time, had been like a release. More than a release actually, it was knowing that all she had to do now was make different decisions and her life would be different, better.

Looking skyward she spoke out loud, 'How am I doing, Dad? Am I passing these challenges well? Am I going to win my life back, because there have been some pretty big losses so far, none more than you?'

That last question left her weeping for the loss of such a wonderful man, and all the more determined to remove the poor excuse for a man who was living rent-free in her home.

She knew that her next challenge lay in forgiving the two people who had been compliant in creating her current reality. That would take some time, but at least now she had taken responsibility for her decisions, she felt that she may have made progress. As that thought entered her mind, she felt something brush against her cheek and saw it fall towards the ground. Re-focusing and looking in its direction she saw the beautifully formed pure white feather as if plucked directly from an angel's wing and knew she was on the right path.

'Thanks, Dad,' she said and took a sharp intake of breath as even the mention of him forced salty tears down her cheeks. She missed him so much it hurt.

Chapter 40
October – Halloween

It had been a couple of weeks of reflection for Mandy over the events since March, a mere eight months since her accident and a visit from her grandad who had negotiated for her life and communicated the rules. She would not have any warning; she wouldn't know if it was a challenge or not and she would have no idea how many or how often these challenges would show up. That had certainly been the case so far. Were any of these events' challenges or were they all? How was she doing? Well enough to still be here she supposed.

She was preparing for the autumn school holidays and considering the outfits she would have to buy on a budget this year, that would take some planning and thrift because the shop that had outfits for Halloween were very expensive. She would plan a bit of fun around making their own and baking homemade cakes, the kids would love that.

John was staying out of her way, which was a Godsend. The kids were excited and Angel had moved to Whitby without so much as a kiss my ass, Mother was keeping her informed and that suited her just fine. It turns out that forgiveness is hard and takes time. She was really trying, there were her new vision board and mantras. There were positive statements on post-it notes all around the house which the kids loved reciting with her. She was reading two books at a time and really digging into the depths of self-development, coaching and growth. So, why was forgiveness so elusive?

Thinking it would be easy once she had accepted responsibility, she was beginning to realise that she had a way to go. Today the main actions at the top of the "to do" list were to call Working Tax Credits to advise them that John was moving out on the thirty first of October and that she would be a single mum, working sixteen hours as a cleaner. She would be able to get help with her rent from the housing benefit department and her council tax, as well as an award from tax credits, she would be able to budget then and look at how she could keep dance classes and karate going. It would be tight, but she would find a way.

Her main priority was to find a way to keep her children doing what they loved, make sure they were well fed and had a warm safe roof over their heads. After all, that is all any of us need she considered.

After speaking to the tax credit department, which was actually a really positive experience, she started to look at the options for doing a psychology degree with the Open University. It turned out that once John had gone and all of the benefits were sorted out, she would be able to apply for a full grant for the course. Elated at the thought of having her degree fully funded she began to draft her goals for the next six months. She was feeling positive and filled with hope when she heard a sudden knock at the door.

Glancing through the glass pane she could see that it was Adam her landlord at the door. She had been appraising him about the situation with her and John and had assured him that it would make no difference. He had confided in her that he had never liked John, that he found him lazy and quite rude so there had been no concerns on his part. He had also told her that her neighbours were moving out at the end of October and he intended to carry out some work on the house so there may be some noise.

'Hi, Adam, what can I do for you?' Mandy asked opening the door fully.

'Oh, hi there, Mandy, I hope you are well. I just wanted to invite you and the kids to the Halloween party at the house. We are having a fancy-dress ball, with fireworks and a full buffet with a prize for the best fancy dress. We would love to see you all.'

Mandy was a bit taken aback. They had never been invited to the big house before, maybe he felt sorry for the kids with their dad leaving, and actually, it would be really good for them. Becca would love it, she wasn't so sure about Dan, he really struggled in social situations with his autism so she might have to make allowances.

'That would be really lovely, Adam, Becca will definitely come, but I am not sure about Dan as he struggles with his autism, you know,' Mandy replied politely.

'Well, why not drop Becca off, she will be fine with my girls and you can take Dan somewhere and pick her up later? We are also having a bonfire and fireworks on the fifth of November and inviting the entire village, we feel it is our duty as Christians, you know,' Adam stated in a very empathic manner; he was so nice.

'Oh wonderful, we will definitely be there, thank you so much for the invites!' Mandy exclaimed with much joy.

'Just being neighbourly, I am more inclined to be so now I know that your husband won't be here, Margaret and I do want you and the children to be happy.'

With that final statement, he bid her goodbye and strode off towards the manor house.

See, not everything has to be bad, does it? she thought to herself and returned to her goal setting still feeling inspired. In no time it was school pick up and off she went to take up her position at the school gates and join the school ground click of parents. It had taken her a while to break into this country click, but once she had, she had discovered some amazing women, some of which had become friends and then there was Ni.

Ni was this funny, potty mouthed Dundonian, who lived in one of the poshest homes in the village. She was a complete enigma and did not give a hoot about what people thought about her, and Mandy loved her. Her ex's mum had won seventeen million pounds on the Euro Millions and bought her the house and given her cash to keep her and her three granddaughters in a nice place. But Ni was just Ni, a one in a million find and she was drawn to Mandy as much as Mandy was drawn to her, they just had fun.

'Has that idiot moved out yet, pal?' Ni had hollered as Mandy walked towards her.

'Nope, he knows the score and I am putting my money on the fact that he hangs around until the bitter end, not that I have any money,' she replied and they both laughed way too loudly.

'Well, he better stay the fuck away from me, asshole. And if he doesn't go, then I will come and kick his wee ass down the road.' Ni's accent was trying to be posh but swearing every other word, Dundonian accent, and was so funny when she was on her high horse.

'Oh, he will go, or his things will be in the cow shed where they belong!' Mandy replied.

'Can I watch? That would be hilarious.' Ni laughed as the school bell rang and the little ones began to line up.

The two friends carried on chatting until all children were collected and safe then went their separate ways to do what mum's do.

Mandy told Becca and Dan about the Halloween party and the Bonfire night celebrations and she had been right about both of them, Becca was excited and Dan didn't want to go. That was fine, she would let them dictate what they wanted to do and she would never push Dan, because to do so, could cause a sensory overload.

Becca already had ideas about her beautiful princess outfit with zombie make up for the fancy dress and Dan decided he would just like ice cream.

All in all, if John left as agreed, Halloween looked like a milestone for positive change.

Chapter 41
October – Charity

It was half term and both kids were full of ideas about all the things they wanted to do. Mandy thought that John might like to spend a bit of time with them before he left, but he was showing no interest in them, only in himself, constantly licking his wounds and seeking sympathy. She had no time for him at all.

Deciding to just get on with a schedule of fun, Becca had drawn up her list. Unfortunately, at the top was, "buy an amazing princess dress". This felt bad. Never before had Mandy had to say no to her children, and although it wasn't a life-or-death item, it was really important to Becca. There was no way she could afford to allocate funds to a dress when she really needed some rainy-day money for the car. Having set a strict budget for the week, it did not include a new dress.

'Becca, I have a really fun idea for your dress,' she said in an animated upbeat way to her daughter.

'What is it, Mum, tell me!' exclaimed Becca, totally engaged.

'OK, sometimes the dresses you buy for Halloween are really common, everybody could buy the same one from the same shop, and I was thinking we should try the charity shops to see if we can find an amazing one-of-a-kind dress that nobody else will have. It would be like a treasure hunt, and I could alter it to fit you. How does that sound?' she offered tentatively.

'Oh my God, Mum, that would be so awesome. I could be totally different from all of the other girls and I might win!' Becca oozed, and Mandy exuded a big sigh of relief.

'So, let's put that on the list as our main task for tomorrow,' she said.

Becca pulled out her red crayon and wrote across the top of their list of activities: "FIND MY PERFECT DRESS."

'Can we make cakes now?' Becca asked.

'Yeah, cakes, Mum,' Dan added.

So, they made cakes, lots and lots of cakes.

The next day having walked the dogs around the triangle and done some nature spotting and gathering, they set off into town. Mandy was hedging her bets that there would be a dress in at least one of the five charity shops that would cost pennies compared to the thirty-pound price tag on the new ones. With a budget of ten pounds a day for the week, she had fed them well before leaving and hoped they could last until they returned home with the snacks she had in her bag. Her back-up plan was to swing by Nana's house on the way home and let her fill them up before setting off for home.

They were in the third shop having had no luck in the first two. Dan was a bit bored but had found the toy section so was happy for a few minutes. There seemed to be nothing catching Becca's eye, so Mandy went to talk to the shop assistant.

'Excuse me, we are looking for an amazing princess dress for Halloween for my nine-year-old daughter. Her dad is leaving at the end of the week, we are on a budget and she really wants to be the belle of the Halloween party, can you help?' Mandy whispered, feeling a little ashamed at having to plead poverty.

'Leave it with me, love, I know how it is, I had four, all grown up now mind,' was the unexpected reply as the assistant shuffled into the back room.

Why had she forgotten that good communication could be your best friend? As a manager she knew resolutely that even poor communication was better than none, she had preached this message to all of her teams. So, why had this not stayed with her? Maybe it was just brain fog from the events of the last few months? Lesson re-learned, if you don't ask you don't get!

The elderly assistant was back with the most stunning red sequined dress that Mandy had ever seen. This was a dress that would blow all other contenders out of the water, and as she turned towards Becca all she saw was a little girl, with wide saucer eyes, mouth agape and pointing her finger towards the dress.

'That one, Mum, please, it has to be that one!' she shouted.

Mandy turned to the assistant and asked, 'How much?'

'To you, love, because I think this dress was made for that little girl, you pay two pounds.'

Tears welled in her eyes, the assistant noticed and quickly saved her from the kids noticing by inviting her to the counter.

'I've been there, love; I know how hard it is and what men are like so this is my gift to you. Pull yourself together and just go and enjoy your day, we will add fifty pence for the little man to choose a toy and you are set.'

Bundling the dress into a bag the assistant shouted over to Dan, 'Since your sister has the best dress in town then you can choose yourself a toy.'

Dan's eyes lit up and he went immediately for the Bob the Builder machine to shore up his already extensive collection.

'I can't thank you enough,' Mandy said, with a full heart and genuine gratitude.

And there it was. She had been searching for an answer to the problem of forgiveness and gratitude and here it was. It was in the small things that are done from a place of kindness. This was her answer; this was the work that needed to be done. That was her activity for the evening secured once the two rug rats were in bed. She would search and she would find.

Leaving the shop with a full heart, having already decided that once her life had changed, she would always support animal charities, after all, it made sense, being such a huge dog lover. What had happened in this small charity shop today had made a memory, not just a moment.

Thanking the woman again and waving goodbye with two very happy children in tow, she headed for her mum's house.

Five minutes later, her two very happy children were excitedly running up their nana's path with their prizes in their hands.

As they burst into the house, Mandy was still only halfway up the path when she heard, 'Nana, Nana, look at this, isn't it the most beautiful dress in the world? This has been the best day ever!'

'Look at mine, Nana, I have a truck, look, look!'

Two pounds and fifty pence and the same in petrol. Who needed money?

Her mum was smiling ear to ear when she entered the room with both children, a dress and a truck draped around her. What a sight to behold.

'We thought we would call on the way home; we have had a very successful day,' Mandy said grinning.

'I see that; do you want a cuppa? How about some pop kids and a brownie?'

Two high pitched yesses and a yes please were her replies.

'Thanks, Mum, I knew you would have a cake of some description and they needed a fill-up. I have managed to only spend two pounds fifty today, thanks to a really nice lady in the charity shop so it gives me more for another day and I didn't want to waste it on food,' Mandy confided.

'Are you managing now that you have nothing left, love? Because I can help, you know,' Rita offered with genuine love.

'I am fine, I have to get all of us used to living on a budget and there is no better place to start than a school holiday week. You know, I am always fine; I am just trying to find a new normal. Listen, if you come across any cleaning work anywhere, will you let me know because I could do with just a few more hours that I can fit in while they are at school. That would be a great thing for you to do for me, help me to help myself,' Mandy asked.

'I hate the fact that you have to do this now because of that idiot and your sister,' her mum responded shaking her head in disgust.

'Look, it was my choice to help Angel and I chose to marry John, so, I can't blame anybody but myself.'

There it was again, the more she said it, the easier it was to swallow.

'How is our kid, anyways, she just isn't speaking to me at the minute?'

'Oh, she is fine, you gave her the money as always, I am her guarantor, she has moved in, the place is a pigsty but I am leaving her to get on with it and lick her wounds,' Rita responded.

'Well, that makes two of them licking their wounds. John is feeling very sorry for himself. I think it may have dawned on him what he is losing, but it is so far past too late now. He will be gone in six days and I am counting the minutes!' she replied.

'Don't ever go back to him, will you?'

'I won't. I am staying on my own for a long time. I have a lot to learn and I want to take my time and focus on the three of us and the dogs. I will come out the other side better, you know.'

'I have no doubt about that!' her mum said with pride and confidence whilst being interrupted by little voices shouting, "Where are the brownies? Where are the brownies?"

They all tucked into nana's homemade brownies, which were definitely up to their usual standard of excellence and had fun playing domino's and drawing pictures.

After an hour Mandy had to be firm in saying, 'Right, kids, it's time to hit the road, the dogs will need a walk and you have way too much sugar in you!'

'Noooooo, ten more minutes! Just ten, please, Mum.' Becca pleaded.

'OK, then we have to go. Before I forget, Mum, do you have any empty jam jars with lids? I know you usually save them. I thought we might go bramble picking tomorrow because there are millions of them on the triangle then we can make some jam and bramble crumbles,' Mandy inquired.

'Yes, bramble picking, can we, Mum, pleeeease?' Becca was excited about everything at the minute.

It had never occurred to Mandy that she had just never had time to do any of this with them so regularly before and they were loving every little thing. Time was precious and the lessons kept coming.

'Yes, I have loads of jars. I will just get them for you. Oh, and Ray has put you a carrier bag of leeks, courgettes, tomatoes, cucumbers and potatoes together out of the garden and greenhouse. And who would like to take the rest of the brownies I wonder?'

Two hands shot up and lots of me, me, me's filled the room. She knew her mum was helping without handing over money because Mandy wouldn't take it, and she was grateful for that. She would be able to make at least three days' meals from those veggies and involve the kids, it was a real gift.

Off they wobbled down the path, laden with brownies, veggies, jam jars and half of the contents of her mum's kitchen cupboards disguised as "things she would never use". She truly loved her mum, and this was priceless versus the events of the last eight months, she was re-learning so much.

They headed off full of smiles and singing the wheels on the bus all the way home.

Chapter 42
October – Brambles

They had arrived home at about four on the first Saturday of the holidays and unpacked their treasure trove of goodies from their day out. The dogs were ready for their walk so off they set around the triangle again spotting all of the brambles they would pick the following day. As they walked, they discussed what Nana had given them and what they would like to have for tea, eventually agreeing on a tomato and cucumber salad, Granddad's potatoes and a tin of salmon from nana's cupboard mixed with mayonnaise. A little bit odd for October, but the weather was still sunny and warm so Mandy would make the most of it. Normally, Dan wouldn't eat salad, but because he was involved in the decision and it was from Grandad's garden, he was really up for it. Another lesson. He had eaten every last bit and said it was the best tea ever, followed by even more brownies. They would sleep well tonight with full bellies, job done for day one.

When they were fast asleep, having had an extended story about Super Jet, Super Ozz, Super Dan and Super Becca who had saved the local town with nothing but Nana's mega brownies, and been rewarded with giant sausages, which Super Jet had greedily guzzled down, Mandy tiptoed downstairs to think.

Reflecting on the lessons of the day, she felt a need to really learn, not just because it may be a challenge set for her to do so, but because that was her natural state. Being a lifelong learner was a gift and a burden at the same time. It had set her apart from her peers because she liked to understand the human side and think creatively, bolstering herself with knowledge, but it also made people feel uncomfortable around her. Now was no different, in fact, she didn't think that wanting to learn new things would ever stop, which is why the prospect of having the Open University degree funded was so exciting. Always a book worm, from two years old so her mum had told her at every opportunity, she had been a bit of a quiet introvert, the fat kid that knew everything. But her intelligence without being a geek had won friends. In fact, in later years, she discovered that her taste in music in being Led Zeppelin's biggest fan and a bit of a hippie had made her popular, with people seeming to want to be near her and follow in her wake. Having the brain and creative thinking ability with her artistic tendencies she had quickly worked out how to lead and motivate people, reward them, boost their confidence and self-esteem and create a loyal team. This had skyrocketed her to the top in her company and resulted in her being headhunted twice.

However, this year was different, because the manager appointed to the store after her accident was female, and not being there to be indispensable and work with her had made her disposable instead. She understood that also, you were only ever as good as the last thing you did at work, and if you are not there to do anything then the writing is on the wall. She could forgive that and own it.

The first part of the forgiveness journey was underway. And with that new knowledge and recognition, she felt tired.

Just as she was about to go up to bed, John walked in. A little surprised to see her still up he looked down and grunted.

Taking this opportunity to help her to understand forgiveness in this context she said, 'Look, John, I know none of this has been easy. I know that you are feeling crap about your choices, and I also know you love your children, so let's just get through this week in the best way we can for the kids. You are not a bad man, you have been overshadowed by me for years, I understand that and I am sorry, but I would just like to end this marriage with dignity and make sure that the kids are still allowed to love us both. What do you say?'

He looked totally stunned and sat slowly down at the table next to her.

'I really want to do that, I know that I am not good enough for you, that is what drove me to someone else, but I do love the kids. Can I spend the morning with them before work?'

It had worked! That little bit of kindness today had passed on and it worked. By being kind and taking some of the load she had managed to improve a difficult situation, this was a great lesson indeed.

'Of course, you can, we are going bramble picking after lunch so it would be good for them to spend some time with you and tell you what they did today.'

By the time she had finished talking he had grown about an inch in height and was smiling.

'Let's talk about practicalities at a time that we are less tired, deal?'

'Thanks, Mand, I really appreciate that.'

On that note, she went to bed, with both dogs in tow and a little man already sprawled over most of her bed in the star-shaped position that only children have.

The next day was beautiful again, and Mandy couldn't believe her luck that they had planned to go bramble picking and it was nice enough to actually do it. While the kids spent the morning telling their dad about their best day ever and having a bit of fun watching a Disney film, Mandy set about finding containers to collect brambles in. She knew they would need a lot because there were millions of brambles to be had, so three buckets were cleaned and laid out in the utility room.

After lunch, two bouncing children and two equally bouncing dogs set off around the triangle ready to start their great foraging adventure. Normally, there was a shortcut they would take so that the triangle wasn't too big. Its actual size was a total of around four miles, too much for the little boy's legs, but today they wanted to go to the far corner where the best brambles were. So, with destination set, they charged on popping every ripe bramble into their buckets. The pickings at the far corner were amazing, but they were about a mile and a half from the house and Mandy was concerned about having to carry all three buckets home. But the young foragers were not to be deterred so they ploughed onwards. The weather had been kind today and it was such a pleasure being outside, but just as that thought entered Mandy's head, she heard thunder.

'What was that, Mum?'

'That, Becca, was our cue to start for home because do you know what follows thunder?'

'Lightening?'

'Yep, and then what?' Mandy prompted.

'Erm, rain.'

'You got it, we have a long walk home and none of us wants to get wet, do we?'

'I suppose not, but we are having fun, this is the best day ever.' Becca pleaded.

And at that moment, just as Becca's words had come out of her mouth, the heavens opened. Mandy had never seen rain like it for years, it was good old-fashioned rain. There was nothing they could do but laugh, and splodge home with buckets swimming with rainwater and brambles floating on top.

As they arrived at the house, Mandy ushered them into the utility room, stripped both kids and sent them upstairs to get dry and put their jammies on.

Placing the buckets on the kitchen bench to sort out later she dried the dogs and peeled her own clothes off. Heading upstairs wrapped in a towel she could hear the laughter from her children, and hear them saying how that had been so exciting and scary.

Putting her own PJs on and heading back downstairs, she shouted, 'Who is up for a Disney movie and some hot chocolate with marshmallows?'

She lit the coal fire and waited for the excited kids to burst through the door.

'Right, you guys, pick a movie and no fighting, while I go and get the hot chocolate. Who wants brownies?'

'Me, me, and lots!' was the exuberant response.

So, while the kettle was boiling Mandy drained the brambles and left them in the sink to dry. *At least they had been given a good wash,* she thought. Putting all of the clothes and towels into the washer first she then made three mugs of hot chocolate and a plate of brownies and carried them through on a tray. The fire had taken and the room was warm. Their hair was drying with the heat and they cuddled on the sofa to enjoy Monsters Inc. again for the one-hundredth time. This would be a memory they were still talking about ten years later. Sensory for Dan it would become one of the best days in his life, which would be one of the only things he would remember from these years.

Chapter 43
October – Dan

How on earth would Mandy ever beat the two best days ever? Thinking about it made her smile. Spending time with her children had surpassed anything that her work life could be remembered for. With the rain still thrashing down and a noticeable temperature drop, she had agreed to start on Becca's dress tomorrow.

Becca had gone to sleep immediately, but Dan was on his second story about the super's and was asking a lot of questions. She had agreed to go to parenting classes after the holidays. Having spent months at occupational therapy with Dan every week, read about ten books and asked thousands of questions, she was sure he was autistic, but nobody was giving her a diagnosis, just possibilities.

He WAS different. He had been late at doing everything in milestone terms, but nobody had seemed overly concerned. He could not use utensils, fasten his buttons or laces nor wipe his bottom. He was struggling with ball sports and the occupational therapist had identified that he had spatial awareness problems. He was quiet, almost in his own world at times and loved playing on Sonic the Hedgehog now he was no longer allowed the older games that his dad had once let him play. He could be lost in "Danland" as they had called it, for hours if he was left to it. He struggled in public places and had a complete meltdown if he was off the ground. The strangest thing that Mandy had noticed so far was that he was a "collector". When Dan liked something, he had to investigate and collect every model, type, toy or whatever it was and he knew everything about each item. They would be displayed by size and colour. He was excellent at jigsaws and very logical in his approach.

Mandy had learned what not to do so that he felt safe but now needed to learn how she could best help her son and keep him in mainstream school. John had struggled to accept that there was anything wrong but eventually had conceded that he could see that there was something. Not that he had ever come to any meetings or therapy sessions.

'Mummy why am I different?' came the little voice that interrupted her.

'You were born special, Son, that is going to set you apart from other people,' was her considered response.

'But boys pick on me and girls laugh at me and I don't understand why?'

'Look, Dan, that happens to everybody, it just feels like it doesn't when it happens to you.'

This was a hard conversation to be having with a four-year-old that she thought was perfect in every way. She wanted to go and shout at all of the other children but knew that would be wrong. She vowed to do her best to be the mum that Dan needed to thrive, no matter what that meant.

'How do you feel right now, Son?' she asked him, to try and distract his train of thought.

'I am happy, Mummy, today was so good. I loved the rain and the hot chocolate,' his innocent reply melted her heart.

Her love for this boy was so strong.

'Are you worried about anything that we can talk about?' she prompted.

'I am worried that I am stupid, Mummy,' he replied with a sad downward look.

'You are not stupid, Son, and I don't want you to think that about yourself. I do want you to promise to talk to Mummy about how you are feeling, especially if you are sad. Can you promise me that?'

'Yes, I can. I love you, Mummy,' was his more confident response.

'I love you more, now shut your eyes and dream of brambles,' she said and he giggled.

Mandy went downstairs feeling like her heart would explode for her son. Knowing better than anyone that kids could be cruel, she had been on the receiving end of that but not as much as her sister had. With that thought, she considered her sister and if it was a possibility that Angel was on the spectrum, then dismissing it immediately as her sister was definitely a victim of mental illness, a terrible affliction. But what if Dan grew up without the right help? Maybe he would feel like Angel did about herself. There was so much self-loathing and feeling worthless, what if Dan felt like that when he was growing up? What if he felt second best? This was the very prompt that Mandy had needed to start to really forgive her sister. Looking at things differently and trying to feel it from someone else's perspective made it much easier to just accept the bad behaviour. But, like her son would need to have, Angel needed some boundaries in place so that she could stop making the same mistakes and hurting people. Tough love. Mandy knew that there was a rough ride ahead with her son, but that there would also be joy and rewards at the end. What the journey would be like with her sister, she had no idea, but the starting point had to be forgiveness. If she could love Dan for what he was, then she needed to do the same for every other person on the planet, including Angel.

Dan was teaching her so much about life and love, but mostly about the infinite possibilities that lay behind each and every human on the planet. This was just the start of their autism journey.

As she turned on the TV to try and relax a little, her mind turned to Louise and she made a mental note to pop over for coffee after the holidays. Less than an hour later she was asleep on the sofa and didn't move a muscle until Jet decided to lie on top of her. Realising she was in his space, he would sneak onto the couch at night, she took herself off to bed feeling groggy but relaxed and slid into the covers next to her son.

She lay there and looked at his little face in the moonlight that was seeping in through the curtains, and she readied herself for the trials and tribulations that lay ahead. If this was a challenge, she was guaranteed to win because she would fight tooth and nail for the right thing for this little man. Nothing and nobody would stop her in her tracks in the fight for the best for him, he was Dan the man, who drives a van, when he can, and he was her superstar! He was Super Dan.

Tomorrow was dressmaking day, so they would come up with something to include Dan. But for now, she needed sleep, it had eluded her for way too many nights since March. Soon there were pleasant dreams of hope and abundance.

At this point in her life, Mandy had no idea how long this journey with autism would be, nor how hard she would have to fight, all of that would unfold. No mother would ever be so ready for the fight than she was at this moment.

Chapter 44
October – Exit

Dressmaking was a real success and the red sequined dress looked amazing now it actually fit Becca, she was strutting around the house like a supermodel. Dan had helped and made a red sequined "super cape" for his story character and he was proud as punch and felt genuinely super. Even the dogs had red super collars made from the scraps, but they were less impressed.

'Since it's still raining, Mum, can we make cakes again? Please?' pleaded Becca.

'You guys have lived on cake this week!' Mandy replied, secretly relieved because they were cheap to make and kept the kids happy on rainy days.

'But cake is so good, Mum,' Dan added, with big saucer eyes.

'I think we will make cakes, and then how about making a homemade quiche for tea?'

Mandy was thinking on her feet with what ingredients were in the house from her mum's gift of food as there was only fifty pence in her purse and it was staying there. Having worked out her daily budget and attempting to hold onto it as long as possible so that if the weather improved, she could take the kids out for a real treat later in the week.

'Cheese and onion quiche, Mum, please, that is my favourite,' Becca piped up.

'With beans,' added Dan.

'That sounds like a plan to me, go and wash your hands and take off your dresses and capes and let's get started,' Mandy replied, and both kids shot upstairs to get ready to make the mess that was inevitable in the kitchen.

Mess definitely did ensue but great fun was had in that kitchen for a good couple of hours.

Disney films, thank goodness for Disney, Mandy thought to herself. Settling all human and hairy children with the fire lit, film on and cakes in hands in front of the TV, she cleaned up the mess.

Whilst she was cleaning and loading the dishwasher, John arrived home.

'Oh hi,' she said politely, but in a distant way, which was just how it was now.

'Hi, I have some good news,' he replied.

'Really, what's that then?' was her hopeful response.

'Mother has agreed for me to move into her house at last. I am going to start packing up my stuff and take some over tomorrow and then I am hoping to be moved out by Friday.'

It was his very sad looking offer.

'That is good news, John, we all need to move on now and allow the kids to settle into a routine without you. They need to know where they stand and what will happen next. Perhaps, you could tell them and have a talk to them. I think it would be better coming from you.'

'I will do later, I am off to pack some stuff and load the car first, is that OK?' he said.

'That's fine, they are watching a movie anyway.'

Off John went upstairs, without even saying hello to his children, and it took Mandy everything in her not to jump up and down with joy at the news, but as always, she contained herself and carried on. That moment would be savoured after he had actually gone.

Maybe there should be a little sadness, but there was none. He had been a poor husband and an even worse father. Although she knew that he loved his children, he just could not be bothered to parent or play with them. He had no real interest in their education, how Becca was doing at dance nor how Dan was doing at occupational therapy for that matter, he just never asked. It was like he was in his own world, just like Dan at times.

I wonder if autism is hereditary?

Once again, Mandy had no idea the fight that was ahead of her in trying to encourage an absent father to take some interest in his children. It was so easy for men to walk away from the responsibility and cost of raising children and this was just the beginning of this particular challenge.

John popped in to see the kids once he had packed the car and told them he was leaving on Friday. When his children asked if he was going to take them out somewhere before he left, they were informed that he didn't have time because he had too much to do. Mandy could see the disappointment on their faces and knew that it had been a good move to save her money on the rainy days so she could take them somewhere exciting on Friday while John made his final exit.

'Good riddance to bad rubbish,' was what her grandad used to say, and she was sure he was saying that at this very moment.

Mandy did what all mum's do instinctively and went to her children with some fun suggestions and uplifted their mood.

'How about we make some bramble jam tomorrow, you two?'

'That would be awesome, Mum!' was the excited response from both of her children.

'And I was thinking we could create some art pieces, I have loads of old wallpaper leftover and we could do some really big paintings on that, what do you think?'

'YAY, you are the best mum ever!' Becca shouted with a big smile on her face, but Dan still had sadness in his eyes.

Mandy thought that his dad leaving was going to be harder for him to understand and he would need to have some talking time over the next few days.

'Well that sounds like a great plan, now what would you really love to do on Friday if I said we could go out for the day?' Mandy asked them both.

'Swimming!' shouted Becca.

'Yes, swimming then MacDonald's,' added Dan.

'Then that is what we will do, no splashing me mind,' she said with a twinkle in her eyes, and both kids responded spontaneously, "Loads of splashing, Mum!"

Gathering her prized possessions, they went for a long walk in the rain before tea. When they returned the quiche was ready and they all changed into their jammies for tea while Mandy heated up the beans and a good hearty meal was eaten on a meagre budget. Everything was possible and this had been the best few days she had ever had with her children. No work, no arguments with John, no demands from her sister, just fun, real fun. Feeling content and more positive about the outcome of her challenges, she noticed a sense of control returning.

Tuesday saw fifteen jars of bramble jam created and three very large paintings of Super Jet and Ozz, and Super Dan and Becca, Michelangelo had competition. Wednesday was more of the same and Thursday brought a break in the weather, a small food shop and a visit to Nanas for lunch.

Friday was awkward really. While John was packing the last things into his car the kids seemed indifferent one minute and asking questions the next. Their father was not being very communicative so Mandy made the decision to just go swimming.

'Let's get our swimming gear sorted and head off now,' she instructed, and a spark of life and joy was visible immediately in her children's faces.

Saying goodbye to their dad, they jumped into the car. This would be a swim that Mandy would be in no rush to encourage them to leave, it would be leisurely and she would stretch it until they were evicted from the pool in the hope that he was gone when they returned. The MacDonald's would be treated like a three-course meal and they would stay there way too long, filling them up and keeping them entertained.

When they arrived home, he was gone, so to distract her children she insisted that they go out with the dogs to walk off the food, it was past five when they set off and she managed to keep them out until six-thirty, having races with the dogs and playing hide and seek. Knowing that returning might throw up some questions, the more tired they were the better.

'OK, let's head home for a big bubble bath and we can all watch a movie together and eat some more cakes.'

'This has been the best week ever, Mum,' Becca said, holding her hand as they walked, 'And, you are the best mum ever, we don't need Dad.'

It was heart-warming, but she couldn't help but wonder how much trauma this would throw up later in life for this little girl. Having not had the best male role model in their lives, Mandy needed to be present and be mum and dad. Knowing she was not alone, her network of friends was more vital than ever now, this was the beginning of a new challenge and winning was everything.

Chapter 45
October – Ni

The Halloween party was the order of the day, it was the last Saturday of the school holidays and that was all Becca could talk about. It was impossible to distract her and she chattered all day about how her make up should look, what time she should be there and what if she won the prize. Never had a nine-year-old girl been so excited about a party. There was however an underlying sadness in her little girl, and it ripped her heart from her chest to see it.

'Do you want to talk about your dad leaving, Becca?' she asked cautiously.

'Why did he lie, Mum?' was the unexpected response.

'What do you mean by that, sweetie? How do you think your dad lied?' Mandy worded her response carefully.

'Well, a few weeks ago I asked him if you guys were going to get a divorce and he said no, that everything was OK, and now he has gone.'

Becca looked really confused.

'Well, that was unfair of him to do that. Sometimes, grown-ups get things wrong and make bad decisions, Becca, that does not mean that you or me or Dan have done anything wrong, it is just what your dad wanted. He was wrong, not you, and you will probably need to forgive him so that you are not mad, does that make sense?'

It was hard to talk to a nine-year-old about grown-up stuff. Mandy wanted to tell her the truth, but she would not understand yet. Vowing to tell her the truth as soon as she was old enough to make sense of it properly, she hugged her daughter.

'It kinda makes sense but I am mad at him because he is not a nice man. He used to leave us on our own all of the time so he could play on his computer, and he used to shout at us all of the time too, you don't shout and you never leave us on our own.'

Becca was sobbing now, she was hurting and angry, this was going to be hard to manage because the answers that were needed would never come.

'Look, you be mad. Punch some cushions, ask your dad why when you see him, but don't keep it inside, OK? Promise me?' was all Mandy could come up with, but inside there was a desire to hurt her soon to be ex-husband for hurting her children, bastard!

'I promise,' came the little voice, 'can we do my make up now?'

'We sure can, go and wash & dry your face and bring my makeup case.'

An hour later there was a very scary looking zombie bride in a red sequined dress with backcombed hair who looked like a character created for a film. Together they had made the monster and discovered that Becca had a real creative talent with make-up.

Lots of photographs were taken and Becca had been and admired herself a thousand times and returned with, 'I think I have a good chance of winning, Mum,' every time.

She was very excited about this party.

'Is it time to go yet, Mum?' every ten minutes!

'Actually, Becca, we will be setting off in five minutes so go and get yourself ready and I will load the car.'

A red flash shot past her at one hundred miles an hour to do last-minute touch-ups and collect her things.

After much negotiation with Dan, Mandy had decided to go over to her friend Naomi's for the evening while Becca was at the party. Dan loved to play with Ni's second-youngest Ali, so the friends could have a proper catch-up and put the world to rights, filling heart and soul up. Ni needed her as much as she needed Ni. Her friend had really had it rough with her ex, who was abusive, narcissistic and manipulative, often using their daughters as pawns in the fight. Although she lived in a beautiful house bought by her mother in law with her lottery win, Ni did not own the house and had foolishly spent all of the settlement money when she had split with her ex, not out of poor choice but out of a deep depression and lack of self-worth that had her trying to fill the void with pretty and expensive things. So now her friend was living on benefits and scraping by with four girls, as a single mum with an abusive ex, there were some days she couldn't even open her front door she was so low, but Mandy loved her and always tried hard to be there when needed. Tonight, was long overdue and she needed to talk to Ni and just relax with her friend. It would be a night of two women trying to work

146

out why men are such dick heads when it comes to their kids, not all men, she knew that, just their men.

Just then Becca wafted down the stairs looking like a million-dollar zombie bride and they all packed into the little Suzuki Swift including the dogs and drove to the big house to drop Becca off.

'Are you excited?' Mandy asked her daughter.

'Yes, Mum, and, I am going to win!'

'Well, whether you do or you don't, you are a winner to me and always will be, you look perfect,' was the proud response.

'I love you, Mum, you are always the best, I love having you home all of the time, so much better than Dad,' Becca said in her usual confident matter of fact way.

'I love being here with you guys, I missed so much, but never again, you are stuck with me now!'

'YAY!!!' in stereo from both of them.

They arrived at the house and Mandy escorted her zombie to the front doors where her landlady Margaret answered the door.

'Oh, my goodness, who do we have here?' she said in an animated way.

'I am the zombie bride,' replied Becca.

'Well, you look amazing, come in and head up to the girl's room, it's up the stairs and follow the noise, they are looking forward to seeing you,' Margaret replied, ushering Becca in the right direction.

'Bye, Mum, love you!' Becca shouted as she disappeared.

'Thanks for this, Margaret, it means a lot, it's been a difficult few days for them, John left yesterday and she is angry. This will at least distract her for the night,' Mandy said with genuine gratitude.

'It is my pleasure, Mandy, I think she stands a chance of winning, that dress is amazing, it must have cost you a fortune?' she pried.

'Had to sell my soul, Margaret, so I sure hope it was worth it!' Mandy laughed, thanked her again, agreed to be back to pick Becca up at eleven and headed off.

This would be so good for her daughter; she was so grateful for her landlord reaching out to help. Beginning to question how many people had held back from offering friendship or help because they didn't like John, maybe she had allowed them to be in a world where people didn't like them both because of how he was, but then they wouldn't offer help now if that was the case. She needed to stop thinking and get to her friend's house. So off they drove on this dark but mild October night, ready to welcome November and colder darker nights soon and also ready for a good belly laugh with her good friend.

As they pulled up to Ni's house the door was flung open and four girls, two dogs, and a rather harassed looking Naomi bounced out to greet them. Unloading her car of one boy and two dogs the entire menagerie crashed back through the front door of the most welcoming home that they would ever have the good fortune to enter. Mandy loved coming here. It was full to the brim with things, mess, toys, kids, animals and good honest love. A refuge for all that were lucky enough to be invited in, for being one of the chosen, she was eternally grateful. Mandy loved her friend but also loved her children just as much. Ni was a fantastic mum, imperfect, but perfect at the same time. Never had she met a more down to earth, authentic loving human and to call her a friend was a gift. They had talked through some tough times together and felt each other's pain, but also shared each other's joy. It was hard to find people of such quality in this life, so Mandy knew that she would always have space for this woman, no matter what happened or where they were in the future.

'Hey, pal, come here and give me a big hug, how the fuck are you and has that wanker gone then?' Ni gushed in that soft and pleasant sounding Dundonian accent peppered with swear words, that always made Mandy smile.

'Yep, he went yesterday thank the Lord!'

It was easy to just be honest and be herself in this wonderful place and with her perfect friend.

'Well that would be a relief for you, hun, but how're the bairns?'

'Let's grab a coffee and a seat and I can tell you all about my week and you can tell me all about yours,' Mandy replied putting the kettle on like it was her own home, and washing a couple of mugs from the massive pile of unwashed pots.

'Sounds like a plan, I will get Indie settled if you are making the coffee.'

And off Ni trundled with her youngest on her left hip as always.

Indie was only two and this was the reason that Ni carried her on even on her worst days. Indie's father was the real love of her life, not her ex, but he had also done a runner, leaving Ni alone with four girls under ten, to two different dads and neither of them worth anywhere near what Ni was. Mandy smiled and thought the two of them should avoid men for the rest of their lives. With two strong coffees in hand, Mandy made her way past the toys and dogs to the living room and settled with her friend.

'So, pal, how are Becca and Dan coping?' Ni asked immediately.

They talked for hours about how neither of them would ever understand how men could just walk away from their children, how hard it was having no money and still trying to do your best for them and how it made you feel pretty worthless and overwhelmed. Deep conversations, sharing personal details that would never be revealed to others, that is the true value of real friends. Not just friends, but other humans that you can trust with your life. There were a few relationships you would have in your life that could go that deep, where you knew that what was said would never be repeated and trust was one hundred per cent there. *Why could neither of these women find a partner that offered the same?* Mandy wondered as they talked, they were good people, loving humans with so much to give. Perhaps this is a question that she would need to seriously consider in order to win back her life. What was missing, what had she done wrong and what needed to change?

The hours flew by in seconds and soon it was time to leave and collect Becca. Sad to be leaving, both friends made arrangements for a catch up the following week when the kids were back to school and off Mandy, Dan and the dogs went to collect the zombie bride.

As they pulled up to the big house, they could see that the party was still going, but it was late so Mandy went to the door and rang the bell.

Adam answered this time.

'Hello, Mandy, as you can see a house full of teens and tweens is a difficult thing to draw to a close, they have had a great time, come in.'

'Thank you, how is Becca?' she asked, hoping that her little girl had enjoyed her night.

'I will let her tell you herself, just wait here and I will get her.'

Mandy waited no more than a couple of minutes for her zombie daughter to arrive with the biggest beaming smile on her face.

'Mum, I won the top prize and Julie has asked me to have a sleepover, can I? Please, please, please.'

'Well, who am I to say no to the winning zombie? Of course you can if that is OK with Adam and Margaret?' Mandy replied looking to her landlord for a response.

'We would love to have Becca stay over, we have a very special breakfast planned in the morning, so why don't you pick her up around 11 a.m.?' Adam said, encouragingly.

'Perfect, have fun, Becca, and no staying up ALL night, love you.'

'Thank you, Mum, I love you, bye,' her daughter responded whilst running back up the stairs.

'Thank you, Adam, I really appreciate this, it is just what she needed.'

'My pleasure, we will see you in the morning.'

He closed the door and went back into the mayhem of screaming children and Mandy smiled from her heart. This meant a lot.

Jumping back in the car she turned to Dan.

'Well, Son, it looks like it's just me and you, so how about a walk with the dogs in the dark and have a hot chocolate, followed by a movie in bed?'

'Can I stay up really late?' was Dan's excited reply.

'You sure can, let's go.'

And off they went with a great plan which resulted in both of them fast asleep with the TV still on fifty minutes later. But they were fifty minutes filled with laughter and joy, so it didn't matter a bit.

Chapter 46
November – Lou

Back to school. This week had flown by but the time with the kids had been absolutely amazing and had taught Mandy a big lesson about what was really important and how much it cost. All the years thinking that she had to be at work all of the time in order to provide the best life for her children had revealed themselves as a lie. The person she had entrusted with their care had proved to be a let-down, money had bought nothing of worth and she had missed moments of value that had been wasted on a self-centred father.

The week had been a lesson and seen much progress, John had actually gone, and she was still here living and breathing, so there must be learning and appropriate reactions, on her part. She was starting to trust her instincts again and go with her gut without overthinking and it felt good. There had been a bit of time now since anything really bad had happened, so maybe her challenges might be smaller and less frequent from now on? Maybe that was part of the plan, bombard her with loads of big stuff then a reprieve to see how she responded, see if she got comfortable. Again, overthinking, there was always the risk that the wrong move would be next so that kept her on edge, and she couldn't tell anyone, couldn't talk about it or share the burden. Despite all of this uncertainty, keeping going was her key objective, and this week with her children had underlined her WHY.

'Right, you two, hurry up and get ready, spick and span for your first day back,' she shouted up the stairs to hurry them both up.

'Can we have pancakes for breakfast, Mum?' Becca shouted down the stairs, still on a high from her weekend win and new friendships made.

'Way ahead of you, they are already in the pan that is why you need to hurry up,' was the response.

'YAY!'

This was followed by the thunder of two pairs of feet running down the stairs.

'We love you being here, Mum, don't ever go back to work, Dad never made us pancakes, you are the best.'

Mandy smiled, 'It is amazing what homemade pancakes will do. Come on, they are ready.'

Six pancakes each were consumed before they were in the car and ready to go in plenty of time. Mandy had planned to drop them at school and then head into the town to see Lou at the pub for a catch-up. Lou was as important to her as Naomi, she had taken on a mammoth task with the pub and really helped her out at the worst possible time, taking a personal risk that had been difficult and put her under extreme pressure. This was one of the gifts that friendships and connections could bring in your life, and Mandy was realising that some of these important relationships had slipped whilst in her unhappy marriage and on the work treadmill; determined to rectify this now if Lou needed her, she would be there.

Knocking at the door at around nine-fifteen, it was opened by a sleepy Louise in her dressing gown.

'Did you forget I was coming?' Mandy asked her friend.

'Sorry, love, late night last night with a lock-in, couldn't get rid of them, come in I need coffee,' Lou responded like it was hard work to even speak.

'Let me make the coffee, Lou, go and splash your face with water and I will see you in a few minutes.'

Giving her friend a hug, off she went to make some proper coffee.

Ten minutes later the two of them were sipping hot coffee and chatting about how things were going for each of them.

'I know the brewery think I am some sort of superwoman, but honestly, it is killing me, love, me and Peter are fighting all of the time, the hours are ridiculous and we are both drinking way too much, I need out,' Lou confided in her friend.

'Have you spoken to the brewery at all? You know, I will do whatever I can to help you if that is what you really want,' Mandy replied, really concerned after what Lou had revealed.

'I would speak to them, but I never seem to get a minute and am always too tired. Do you think you could speak to them for me?' Lou pleaded.

'Of course, I will, what do you want to happen, Lou? How quickly do you want to be out?' Mandy asked.

'Like yesterday, love, I just don't think I can hack it anymore.'

'OK, have you looked for somewhere to live yet?' Mandy prompted because she could see that her friend had not thought this through.

'No, not yet, but I could do that today,' Lou said more positively and with more of a spark.

'Right, you look for a house, get down the Job Centre and start applying for jobs and I will speak to the brewery today. Let's work on six weeks as a timescale, because I think that they will want you here for Christmas and that gives them time to find new tenants and you time to find work and accommodation. Let me see if I can get them to help you with bonds and deposits as you have done such a great job. We can sort this, Lou, I will always be grateful for your help and if I can give you something back in return, then it is the least I can do.'

The look of sheer relief on her friend's face was enough feedback for Mandy to know that this was the right thing to do, she would need to use her best-negotiating skills, but Lou deserved to walk away with something and her head held high for the hard work she had done here. Mandy was sure that the brewery would see it the same way, after all, Lou had completely turned their pub around for them in a few short months. Louise had a talent with people, problem-solving and focus, she just gave way too much of herself in the process. Her friend deserved to get that back and have a chance of happiness with her man.

Leaving Lou with a hug and a smile on her face, Mandy headed home to call the brewery. Two hours later she was on the phone to Lou to tell her that they had agreed to all terms and were going to pay her friend a thousand pounds for her hard work as a bonus and that she had until the second week in January and then, freedom. Lou cried tears of relief and Mandy nurtured another important relationship by allowing someone that she cared about to be their best version of themselves.

Sitting at home that afternoon with a couple of hours before collecting Becca and Dan from school, Mandy decided to take stock and do a bit of brainstorming. It was November and over the last eight months she had almost lost her life and been given a second chance, she had lost her beloved dad, her husband, every penny she had, her relationship with her sister and was still suffering pain from her injuries. On the other hand, she had completed three diplomas', discovered and studied the book "The Secret", nurtured good friendships and family connections, kept going despite wanting to give up and re-discovered the joy of spending time with her children. It was time to really try and focus on forgiveness and gratitude because although she had lost so much, she had also gained. Her ability to remain positive had been what had set her apart in her job, her ability to always use her creative skills to generate new possibilities and regain control and focus, was serving her well in life now and she was ready to really think about her path forward. It was time to start sketching out a strategy, but she decided that the first thing that needed to be worked on was her own mindset to open up her creative thinking and generate ideas and solutions. She was going to say yes to every opportunity and see where it led, right or wrong this would teach her some lessons.

Chapter 47
November – Progress

Now officially a single parent, with a low income, Mandy had discovered that she could seek support from Working Tax Credits, Housing Benefit and could apply for Disabled Allowance for Dan once he was diagnosed. This all felt quite embarrassing for her having been in such a highly paid job, but she would do anything for her children and had braved the humiliation at the bankruptcy court so she made the calls and sent off the applications. The guidelines allowed her to be self-employed and work sixteen hours a week and still claim all of these benefits so at least there was a starting point. Currently, she had three cleaning clients that amounted to twelve hours so there was the opportunity to take on another four-hour shift as a minimum. It was hard work, but it was work and again she was prepared to do anything to support her children.

Drawing up a strategy that facilitated her to only work sixteen hours, because her children needed her, working any more than that and she would end up paying for childcare now that her status was "single parent". John had been dumped by the woman he was seeing and he had phoned her in a pathetic attempt to allow him back telling her that he still loved her, she had told him he was delusional and to fuck off and he was now punishing the kids by not coming to see them. He was also on every dating site desperately trying to find a replacement and that was his main focus, so there was no chance of any help there.

Deciding that she just needed to live within her means and be the best cleaner on the planet and just get on with it, that was a start. It was her own business so she was not working for minimum wage, knowing the value of excellent and reliable service enabled her to charge a premium price for the work she was doing and all of her clients had come to her so far. If there was one thing that she knew, it was that you get back what you put in, so she was prepared to hold her nerve and see what happened for the sake of the kids.

It only took a couple of weeks for her benefits to be in place and once the first payments had been received there was a feeling of ease and relief that came over her in that she could pay her bills and work out a budget to keep Becca at dance lessons and Dan at karate. Being good at budgeting, having managed multi-million-pound businesses, this was second nature to her. It was very tight with dance lessons costing over six hundred pounds a term, and karate another one hundred a month, but she could do it, just. There was no chance of any support from John, in fact, he had been shouting his mouth off in his village that he wasn't going to get a job until Dan was eighteen so that he didn't have to pay maintenance, it had gotten back to her as it always does in these small places, but she just shrugged it off like always, after all, he couldn't disappoint her any more than he already had.

Accepting that she was alone in this and could only rely on herself was actually quite a release. Knowing that every action that she took was being observed and judged there was a real need for her to make sound decisions. At that moment wondering if there would be any feedback or signs that her choices had been good, it brought a feeling of anxiety, would it just be revealed to her at some point in the future that she was to remain on the planet and how long would that be? As the thought entered her head, so had a really clear colour picture of her dad. He was happy, healthy and cracking jokes and he just looked at her and nodded as if to say you are on the right track. *Was that a thought or reality?* she wondered. *I must be seeing what I want to see, and now I am talking to myself.*

The ringing of the phone startled her and she hurried over to answer, 'Hello.'

'Ah, hello, is that Mandy?' a male voice enquired.

'It is, who is calling and how can I help you?' she replied politely.

'My name is Trevor and you were recommended to me by one of your clients. I am looking for someone for four hours a week to service my holiday cottage for me. I am a professional and work away a lot so I need a premium and reliable service and have had no end of trouble with agencies. I mentioned it to a friend of mine and your name came up. I am willing to pay twenty pounds an hour for the right person.'

'Well, Trevor, I am delighted to meet you and can assure you that you have just spoken to the right person. I only take on premium clients so the fit seems right. I can start immediately and do not need any instruction. Would you like to set up an interview?' Mandy responded with confidence.

'No, you came so highly recommended and your response tells me everything, you are perfect. Can you start tomorrow?'

'I certainly can, give me your address and details.'

Mandy scribbled down the address, where she would find the key, Trevor's telephone number and that was that. The universe had just delivered exactly what she needed at just the right time, thinking about "The Secret" and about her positive mindset and she made another decision, this afternoon she would create a new vision board.

Chapter 48
November – Pennies

Although the benefits had been paid reasonably quickly and Trevor had turned up at just the right time, the invoice for Becca's dance lessons had landed in the second week of November. Becca had also grown out of her ballet, modern and tap shoes and needed replacements so there was a hefty bill for over seven hundred pounds to be paid by the end of the month. Trevor was paying monthly on receipt of her invoice and Dan's karate was also due at the end of the month. Mandy took a sharp intake of breath and sat down to look at this month's finances, knowing that overall, there was just enough, but this was going to test her in a way she had not been tested before. There was only just enough income to cover outgoings and next month there was Christmas to consider. Her rent was paid and not due again until the first of December so her housing benefit would cover that. On paying these bills, she would have a maximum of sixty pounds a week over the next two weeks for petrol and food. That was beyond tight for the three of them and two dogs. There would need to be some real penny pinching for a couple of weeks, but there was no real choice. There was no way she was going to plead poverty at Becca's dance school so she wrote a cheque for the invoice and put it in an envelope, she did the same for Dan's karate and took a breath. This was her challenge for this month, budgeting to the penny and coming up with ways to generate some additional income.

Deciding that the challenge was achievable and that it would teach her a lesson she sat down to create a meal planner. Firstly, taking stock of everything in the cupboards, freezer and fridge and then looking at what meals could be made and for how many days with what she had. It was only fifteen days to the end of the month so a fifteen-day plan of three meals a day and snacks, including dogs was required. This was the only time in her life that she had needed to do this but approaching it with the same precision planning that had been successful at work, was how the problem would be solved. If she could plan an entire budget and staff establishment and meet targets in all key indicators in business, then this would be a piece of cake and her children wouldn't even notice.

It turned out that there was enough to make evening meals for eight days with what they had in, she could bake cakes and make pancakes four times with the kids so they would think they were abundant. Twenty pounds a week was necessary for petrol to do just school runs, dance and karate runs, and seven pounds for dog food. That left her thirty-three pounds a week to buy food for the three of them, that was doable.

There was not a single doubt that this was achievable and that December would come and go with all of her bills paid and money in the bank. Planning a very strict budget for Christmas would deliver enough to treat the children well. Feeling empowered and really motivated her intent was set.

Collecting the children from school she informed them that they were going to do a challenge for the month to see how much money they could save and then set them the task of sorting through their toys and clothes to see if there was anything they could sell. Mandy went through her own wardrobe as well, and they ended up with the dining room half full of toys, clothes, shoes, jewellery and odds and ends.

'Why are we doing this, Mum?' Becca asked.

'Because I want to have a clear out before Christmas to make room for all of the new things that you will get from Santa,' Mandy replied.

That was all that needed to be said, talk of Christmas started both of them chattering about present lists and what they wanted. Mandy gave them the task of writing only the five things they really wanted on their list and if they added one, they had to take one away each time. This worked really well and was much easier than imagined, her children were enjoying being coached and were included in decisions.

Having generated so much excess stuff, the plan for tomorrow, while they were at school, was to put the lot online and get it sold. Calculating that this could generate at least a hundred pounds and would go directly into the Christmas fund, not to be touched for anything else, a sense of ease came over her.

Setting these tasks and facing the problem head-on had generated lots of creative ideas in her head and she was busily brainstorming things they could do for free, and things they could make. Setting the intention of spending the next two days outside of work getting a firm plan together and involving the kids, she felt completely motivated to turn this around. What a great lesson indeed.

Chapter 49
November – Network

Sitting at Ni's house for coffee immediately after the school run Mandy was chatting about the exercise she had done with her finances and the excess clothing and other items, and Ni was mesmerised.

'How the fuck dae you come up with this stuff pal? I canny get from one-week tae the next without overspending. You are so fucking clever.'

'Don't be daft, I am the same as everyone else. I am just using the skills I learned in work to manage my life, it's nothing special,' Mandy replied to her friend genuinely.

'No, pal, it really is a special skill ye have, I know loads of women who struggle tae manage I bet they would love some advice,' Ni responded.

'Well, why don't you arrange a coffee morning for them and I will come along and do a coaching session and give them some free handouts that will help them with their planning, I will even bake some cakes from my store cupboard and share some cheap recipes,' Mandy offered, realising instantly that here was a gap and an opportunity to expand her current network.

Ni went to lots of toddler groups with Indie and had a whole different group of friends to Mandy, just as Mandy had a whole different group at dance and karate. This was a great opportunity to get some practice at running workshops, get some feedback and make some new friends. What an exciting opportunity from just having a conversation and sharing some learning. There was some mileage in this.

Ni was so enthusiastic to get involved and it really lit her up, starting to look at dates immediately she was really excited to tell all her friends about it. Giving her some more of the detail Mandy realised that this really was a skill that could be shared to help other women and the seed was planted. Say yes to every opportunity, no matter how seemingly insignificant and see where it takes you.

Leaving to go to her cleaning job Mandy left Ni with a list of the best days to do her workshop and the friends hugged excitedly knowing that one conversation had changed both of their days.

Returning home after her job, as usual, there was only an hour to walk the dogs, grab a bite to eat and head back out for the school run then dance and karate classes. Picking up the mail as she came in despite the enthusiastic greeting from two very excited dogs, she noticed a package. Throwing it on the table with the rest of the mail off they went for their walk.

Once back at home she swiftly made a sandwich, a cup of tea, grabbed a packet of crisps and sat down to open the mail. The package turned out to be the first copy of her book. The fact that it was going to be available around this time had completely slipped her mind. How odd that this would turn up today when she had just come up with an opportunity to network. Maybe there would be an opportunity to sell the book at the workshops or at least generate some interest. Publishing costs had been paid for and an initial fifty copies of the book ordered prior to the bankruptcy, so those could be sold, once she had confirmed this proof copy was OK, and then it could also be sold online using social media.

Network was important, way more important than had been initially apparent and if she was going to bounce back with her life anytime soon, then there was a need to increase her network. This seemed to be a good strategy for life and for business and would be right at the centre of her new vision board. But for now, it was time for the school run and classes. Having to constantly jump from one thing to another was a real hindrance when there was a need to think and plan strategically, but she would have to find a way to do it if success and abundance were ever going to be present in her life again. Just getting by and planning how to live on pennies was not enough. Although very grateful for what she had and really happy, Mandy hated poverty and did not wish to be caught in that trap for very long.

Knowing that it was possible to figure this out and come up with the solution, no matter how long it took, made her feel more focused.

Chapter 50
November – Friendships

What was really obvious, as opportunities started to appear, was that the mindset that you faced each day with created a chain of events. Mandy was incredibly intrigued by this and ready to fully review what was happening. After such a bombardment of dramatic events that had been painful, hurtful and downright difficult, her heart felt like it was healing a little and as that happened her outer behaviour changed along with it. She felt less worried about the challenges on one hand and then more worried on the other, because this period of calm was slightly unnerving, waiting for whatever would come next. But those moments of worry were becoming less, so her creative side was emerging again with positive and solution-based thinking. This felt completely empowering and she knew in her soul that all that was needed was to keep feeding this creativity with actions that would bring more opportunities.

Taking a piece of blank paper and a pen she started to write down the positive things that were in her life, and the difficulties. The list was about even on both sides and she knew that in order to create more positives it was important to work on mitigating the negative side of the list. When she considered it, it could be related to the knowledge gained after working in retail for so long. When appointed in her very first store manager position, she was also studying part-time for her Management Studies Diploma so was learning the theory and had been given the gift of being able to put it into practice. To be fair, it had been a "token" appointment to let the world see that Somerfield was promoting women into management positions, and having been given an underperforming store with a brief to improve it, that is what her actions delivered. What she knew was that the poor sales performance was a "lag" indicator of all of the other actions that were happening in the store. Deciding upon her appointment to only focus on the "lead" indicators the sales would come. In that environment, the "lead" indicators had been the store team and their motivation; training and recruitment; customer service; marketing and operating procedures. Basically, it was all about people, systems, customer satisfaction, promotion and happiness. It was possible to apply this formula to life and see the same results, this she knew in her head and heart because her first store had become the top-performing store in the company, she had built an amazing team, secured the store as the place to shop in the community and had been promoted after two years.

It was a strategy, and it started with people. No longer surrounded by a team of people but she had a network and a great group of friends, they would be her team. So, how to motivate the team and involve them in helping her to turn her life around and face any future challenges, no matter how difficult, was her top goal.

Having the time to think and create plans was helping her self-esteem, which had been knocked badly this year with all of the events. Even her thinking had been difficult to re-train because of this set of challenges that sat with her every day, not knowing when the end would be, but now there was some light and so deciding to start to create the content for her very first talk to a group of women was a huge motivator. Naomi had managed to book the following Monday for her first talk and there were fifteen women who had said they would come along. This was an amazing start and a really critical piece of research for her in terms of her offer. Having no clue yet what would come of it, but knowing that it was important, her gut was telling her to just do it, so she was listening.

Deciding to keep the content that she delivered to only one theme, and do it well, she started to prepare her talk. How to create a budget, live small but think big. The items that had been put online had generated almost two hundred pounds, which had been a gamechanger for the Christmas budget and was a great example to use, so she would take the cash along to create a visual. Her book was the second visual and motivator, what you can do even when things are tough and she had created a budget planning spreadsheet that was really simple to use. Next to create some recipes that can be made for next to nothing and the talk was good to go. Feeling excited and really positive she set off on the school run and knew her work had to be parked for the rest of the day to focus on dance classes, park visits, cooking dinner and spending time with her children because there was nobody else to do it. All of a sudden, she felt lonely, frustrated and angry at the world because the creative side of her had to be squashed to focus on the needs of her children. How selfish was that feeling? They were really important to her, but the adjustment to being a single mum and the sacrifices that were necessary were proving difficult. Driving alone to school, tears rolled down her face. This was going to be an internal battle filled with guilt, love and frustration and maybe a lot harder than it had first appeared. She needed to talk to someone and was so pleased to see Naomi at the school gates. Walking towards her friend the tears started to prick her eyes once again.

'What's up pal?' Ni said quietly and came over and gave her a big hug.

'I am just feeling a bit overwhelmed and guilty for wanting so much but knowing that I am now a single mum and the kids have to come first, it just hit me today,' Mandy replied, wiping the tears swiftly before any of the other mums noticed.

'Mum guilt, pal. We all get it; it takes me down to a place you don't even want to know about,' Ni replied softly.

'How do you deal with the adjustment?' Mandy asked her friend.

'I am the wrong person tae ask, pal, some days I don't even get dressed until five minutes before I get here, I eat biscuits, cake, chocolate and crisps and feel like I can't face the world. Some days I want to give up completely and sleep forever. But I throw some slap on, smile and turn up at these gates and become mum again. It's a fucking fight every day. But you are better than me, you have something, don't waste it, pal. Find a way.' Naomi's words struck a chord and Mandy could feel the tears welling up again and her friend hugged her tight.

'Why don't you all come over on Saturday after all the kid's classes, bring the dogs and some booze and sleepover? We can have a proper natter, have a drink and relax,' Ni offered, with obvious love and complete selflessness.

'I love you, pal, and that would be perfect,' was Mandy's response, just as the school doors opened and the sound of excited children filled the air.

What would she do without this woman? Mandy thought, *this was probably the most important relationship in her life right now.* The importance of friendships and the value they bring.

'Take your time with this, Mandy, you have a lot to learn,' she said to herself, just as her little bundle of happiness ran towards her and gave her the biggest hug.

Chapter 51
November – Expectations

What an awesome weekend they all had at Ni's. The kids had all played together well and been almost self-sufficient because there were so many of them. They had been able to walk the dogs, make themselves food and snacks and entertain themselves while the two friends had opened a bottle of wine, or two, that Ni had found at the back of the cupboard and it had gone down a treat. Mandy hadn't realised just how hard it was for her friend until she had stayed overnight. Naomi's eldest had mental illness problems, yet undiagnosed, which meant that she was prone to aggressive outbursts that included smashing furniture and hurting herself. Ni was fighting to get her diagnosed and the system was coming up short. All of the girls were vulnerable because of their dad's confusing, manipulative and aggressive behaviour and Ni had to deal with the backlash of this as well as living in poverty in a big expensive house. No wonder she struggled, but it really did put things into perspective for Mandy. No matter how hard things were for her, she had the knowledge and ability to find a way back out, no matter how long it took or how difficult things were. Her friend wanted nothing more than to have enough to live on and be a good mum. Mandy wanted more than this but had to work out a path.

One of the things that Ni had said to her over the weekend was that she had once had high expectations of life but now just focused on surviving the day. This made Mandy feel really sad that other people and circumstances had made this lovely woman give up her dreams and just concede to survival. With no influence to change her friend's life for her, but with the skills to come up with solutions for herself, maybe when she had succeeded, sharing what had been her lessons could help others.

It wasn't in her nature to give up. Mandy had faced sexism, misogyny, tough targets, now this series of unfortunate events and this hideous challenge she was caught up in, there was no way she was going to lower her expectations of life or give up on her dreams. What she had learned over the weekend was to walk before she could run. Being a single mum meant that there were two children who needed to be her absolute top priority, and also two dogs. It was too soon to think too big just yet, there was still a huge investment in her own learning to make, and a need to be a good role model for those small humans. Life would be focused on encouraging them to have big expectations and dreams and her role would be to lead by example a step at a time. If they were with her on the journey and felt the change maybe they would realise that you can do anything if you put your mind to it, after all, they had seen her be strong through the events of this year, so that was a good start.

Anyways, it was time for her to present to the ladies at the coffee morning, and the village hall where they all attended toddler group had kindly offered the space for her to do the workshop. Mandy had no fancy flip charts or projectors but had lots of old wallpaper and some bulldog clips, so she had improvised and used her creative skills to come up with some fun visuals. Deciding to use her own story from this year, minus the visitation from her grandad and the challenge she was facing, as her introduction, just because everyone has a story, it would lead them to where she was now and why she had to live small, it felt more natural to be telling a story.

Arriving at the hall, Mandy felt unexpectedly nervous. Where had that come from? She had delivered talks and presentations to massive audiences, her own division of twenty-three managers and even to her bosses and never felt as nervous as this. Maybe it was because this was personal and that was business? Whatever the reason, she actually felt sick right now but knew that she needed to put on her big girl pants and just get on with it.

The welcome was a warm one from most, but a couple of the women were looking her up and down in that way that women do when they are sussing out the competition. Ignoring them and thinking how much easier it was to work with men as they were just left-brained, down to business and had testosterone-driven competitiveness, which was clearly visible, was bolstering her confidence. Women could be bitchy and nasty, trying to bring you down because of their own perceived inadequacies, she knew this from being the boss and dealing with both sexes in different ways. Just thinking about her knowledge and experience was enough to knock out the nerves and she settled comfortably into the group.

Delivering the presentation like a pro and encouraging the group to get involved and have a go at some of the activities that had been prepared had been a big hit. They had loved her story, her book and her cakes. Mostly, they had all, even the glaring twins, come over and said it had been the best talk they had ever been to and they would love her to speak again to this group and that group.

'See, pal, I told you that you had something special,' Ni said as the rest of the women left and the friends tidied up.

Hugging her, Mandy replied, 'And you were right, I had forgotten how good it felt to share things with others that can help them, for no other reason other than to pass on skills. A couple of them have taken my number so who knows where this will go, but it won't do any harm. Thank you, pal, when you have so much on your plate, you still helped me. You are a true angel.'

Mandy drove to her cleaning job next and decided to apply a time limit to the cleaning of two years. Knowing that it would take time, it gave her insight as to what needed to be done, and she was formulating a plan. This was possible, even if it was at a much slower pace than she was used to.

Chapter 52
December – Snow

It was the second week in December, only two weeks to go until the kids finished for the Christmas holidays and Mandy had come downstairs, opened the back door to take the dogs for a walk and discovered that it had snowed through the night and it was at least eighteen inches deep. A bit taken aback, she pulled on her wellies and went outside anyway thinking that the kids would be ecstatic but they may not make it to school. The dogs had great fun bounding through the snow and chasing snowflakes, but Mandy had to defrost the snowballs off Ozzy's underbelly and tail when they returned, much to his disgust. Turning on the radio to listen to the local station which reported on school closures due to bad weather, she had her suspicions confirmed, the school was closed and there would be daily updates. She turned on the TV to listen to the weather forecast and the news was not good. The snow was to be persistent now for a few weeks and was to be even worse in the north.

Having bought Christmas presents with the money made from her online sale and saved a bit extra once she had been paid at the end of November and had received all of her new benefits, there was less need to worry. The oil tank was due for a refill this week for winter and this could prove difficult due to the weather and may leave them with no heating in a couple of weeks if the delivery could not make it through. She would get on the phone today and try and sort this out as a priority. In the meantime, there was a need to find somewhere to get stocks of logs and coal for the fire so that there was a backup plan, number two on her list of things to sort out today. There would be no work if the kids were off unless Ni could have them so she had better look at that as well

Wondering if her next challenge was one from mother nature, she decided to just be ready with as many solutions as possible and put everything else on hold. One of the things that entered her head when thinking about the problem that faced her with the weather was her recent re-connections through Facebook. About eight weeks ago she had received a friend request from an old flame that never was. Dave had been her crush during her teenage years and he had wanted her badly, but they had both always seemed to be in a relationship when the other was free so nothing had ever happened. He was currently in a relationship and had reached out as a friend and that suited Mandy down to the ground as she had no interest in men whatsoever. He had however offered to help her in any way that was needed in her role as a single mum and she had thanked him and they had spoken a lot over the last couple of months about music, life and ups and downs, she really valued his friendship. Anyways, Dave drove heavy plant machinery and if they were stuck, he would come to her rescue. Adding him to her list of resources it was time to go and inform Becca and Dan about the snow, that they were off school and that pancakes were on the menu, bracing herself for the squeals of excitement.

Her hunch was correct, there was much squealing and Becca was downstairs in a flash, wellies, coat, hat and gloves on, and before Mandy could even say slow down, she was outside with the dogs and there was a Becca sized snow angel on the trampoline and the makings of the first snowman. Dan followed a couple of minutes behind and Mandy decided just to watch through the kitchen window and make pancakes, it was warmer inside than out and she had only just defrosted from the dog walk. Standing there watching there was a wave of gratitude for this place, it was such a haven. No traffic, only the house next door and the big house to consider and complete peace. Her children could play safely and she could watch over them, it was perfect. So, send the snow, they would cope and they would have fun. Pouring three pancakes into the pan she smiled at the sheer excitement on her children's faces.

With that thought, John came to mind. He had moved to Manchester the previous week to be with the latest internet catch and had not seen the kids because he was "too busy moving". Looking at the weather now, that was all the reason he needed to excuse himself from seeing them at Christmas. Not that bothered herself, she wondered how Becca and Dan would feel facing their first Christmas without their dad. Her job would be to make it extra special.

'Who wants pancakes?' she shouted and two red-faced, snow-covered children appeared in the utility room. 'Put your coats, hats and gloves on the boiler to dry off while you eat your breakfast then you can go back out if you like.'

'Yeah, Mum, we are going to build the best snowman ever and call him, Homer J Snowman,' Becca informed her and they all laughed.

Hot pancakes with lashings of butter and maple syrup set them up for round two. No sooner had they consumed their own body weight, both children were back outside and Homer J was under construction. Mandy loaded the dishwasher, cleaned the kitchen, cleaned out the fire, set a new one and ran the hoover around while the kids played. Then she put on her wellies and coat and went to join them and the biggest snowball fight you can imagine erupted until they were all soaked and freezing. Homer J was complete, photos taken and all three of them were ready for some hot chocolate and a hot bath.

Once they were all dressed the excited children settled in front of the TV while Mum made phone calls. First to Naomi to see if she would have the kids if they were still off school over the next three days so Mandy could work, that was fine and ticked off the list. Next, the oil company, who informed her that there would be huge delays because of the weather but they would get to her as soon as they could and not to worry. Mandy re-iterated that she was a single mum with two children under ten and that the oil supply would run out in two weeks, but was consoled with the assurance that they would be there before it ran out. Next coal and logs, as a just in case, she arranged for a ton of logs to be dropped off and then the same conversation with the coal supplier, they would get to her as soon as they could. Next, she called her clients to assure them that she would be there over the next few days but had the kids off and maybe a little late depending on roads and access, all was fine. Communication was a wonderful thing.

Feeling accomplished at her approach to the day she settled with Becca, Dan and the dogs to watch a film and enjoy this moment in time.

Snow is fun for the first day, but when the next day arrived and there was the same amount again, there was work to get to and Mandy wasn't quite so enthusiastic. Getting the kids ready for the day at Ni's, she started up her little Suzuki Swift and let it warm up before they set off. Her little car had started the first time and was actually surprisingly solid on the road despite the weather. Sailing past other more expensive cars stranded at the side of the road she made it to her destination with no problem. It was not pleasant to drive in but she managed to work, pick up the kids and make it home, picking up shopping and supplies on the way just in case.

It was looking like the school was going to be closed until after Christmas which meant instead of just under three weeks off, the kids would be off for nearly six weeks. That was a long time on your own, pretty much snowed in with limited resources. Every plan that was currently in her mind was instantly wiped out and was replaced with thoughts of survival. The forecast was bad, it was predicted that many rural areas would be snowed in and cut off, there was a red weather warning and everyone was to be prepared. No matter how good you are at coping, the thought of being completely alone with your kids off school, potentially no fuel and the risk of being snowed in is quite daunting. Mandy picked up the phone and called her friend.

'Hey, pal, are you still OK for having the kids tomorrow if I can make it through?' Mandy asked her friend.

'That's nae problem, pal, but I am going, to be honest with you. I am feeling really low tonight. I think it's the thought of being trapped here with the kids and no way out twenty-four seven. It terrifies me,' Ni responded, sounding genuinely down.

'We need to keep each other going, Ni, how can we do that? Can I bring anything over with me? What if I bring the dogs as well, make a casserole and some cakes and then I stop at yours for tea and do something with the entire tribe?' Mandy replied, thinking on her feet about how she could keep her friend sane.

'Ah, my wee saviour, I would love that. Why don't you stay over tomorrow night and then go straight to work from here the next day?'

'That's a great idea and then I could pick up my kids after work and maybe have a couple of yours overnight to give you a break?' Mandy offered.

'Ahh, that would be amazing, you could take T and Ali so that Becca and Dan have someone to play with each and then if I have just two, I can get stuff done,' Ni sounded like a weight had been lifted.

'Right, that is step one of our survival plans then.'

Chapter 53
December – Baileys

Mandy drove over to drop Becca, Dan and the dogs off with Becca holding tightly onto a huge pan of stew and Dan in charge of a large batch of cakes. On the way, she picked up a couple of bags of shopping up and a litre bottle of Baileys. When she arrived at her friend's house to unload her small car of its large cargo, she struggled to get the car up the lane. The main roads were not bad because the gritters had been out, but the lanes and minor roads were a real challenge. On the third attempt, she managed the run-up and parked the car. Ni opened the door and looked like she hadn't slept for a week.

Mandy gave her a hug and asked, 'Are you sure you are OK to do this because I can take them all home and call in sick, I have already spoken to my clients and they all understand.'

'No, pal, it's OK, I have just had a rough night with T, she had a total meltdown and trashed the dining room. She is calm now so all should be OK, I am just knackered,' was Ni's weary reply.

'Well, I will only be gone for four hours, when I get back you can go have a bath, a nap and I will sort tea and kids, and that is non-negotiable. Oh, and by the way, I brought two bags of kid food and a litre of Baileys for the grown-ups, so the day will improve,' Mandy assured her friend.

Naomi's eyes filled up, it was her turn to feel emotional and just as she had been there for Mandy, then Mandy would be there for her. Friendship is like lifeblood when you are a lone parent, and mother nature was magnifying every problem at the minute, but she would not win.

Mandy went off to work navigating the roads as best she could and returned four hours later, weary but very much aware of the job there was to do now.

Entering the house, it was evident how badly Ni was coping so she took Indie and marched her friend off upstairs for a bath with the instruction that she needed at least two hours to get everything organised so Ni was not allowed back down until six and if she fell asleep that someone would come and wake her for dinner.

Gathering the tribe together there was a team meeting in the living room. First, she checked that T was feeling OK and then said that as she and Becca were the oldest that it would be really appreciated it if they could help, T and Becca were great and said they were up for anything. Mandy asked them to take all of the dogs out for at least an hour in the woods, giving them five pounds to treat themselves at the shop and told them to wrap up warm and off they went. Next, there was Jaye, Ali and Dan, they were given a list of things that Mandy thought they could manage like picking up dirty cups and plates and bringing them to the kitchen, putting all of the toys away tidily, removing empty toilet roll holders and filling up with full rolls. Their treat would be sweets that Mandy had bought at the shop, so they were motivated. Next, she cleaned Indie up, changed her nappy and clothes and sat her in her highchair in the kitchen with some toys and snacks and set about washing pots, cleaning up and making dinner. There was a pile of washing to fold so she folded it and then vacuumed through the whole house.

All children performed well and were treated with not only sweets but praise and they asked what else they could do, so more tasks were set.

By quarter to six, the house was shipshape, the dogs were walked, the dinner was made and all children were calm, tired enough to be hungry and Ni was as quiet as a mouse. Mandy left Indie with Becca and T and tiptoed up the stairs to check on her friend. She was sound asleep on the bed. She had bathed and obviously fallen straight asleep. Mandy closed the door gently and crept back downstairs, went into the living room and closed the door.

'Right you lot, house meeting. You have all been absolutely brilliant this afternoon, I am so proud of you. Your mum is fast asleep and I think she deserves to be allowed to rest properly. I have dinner ready so if we all go and eat together in the dining room and keep the noise down, then have a team effort to clean up after, I have cakes with strawberry jam and cream for pudding. We will let your mum wake up when she is ready and watch a film after we have eaten. Is that a plan we can all follow?'

Everyone agreed.

'T, you are the oldest, so I am going to make you the team leader, OK?'

Ni's eldest stood up straight and looked really proud of herself, nodding in agreement.

'That doesn't mean being just bossy, when you are a team leader you have to give the team members a task and then make sure they have done it then praise them if they do it well. My team always work together and I have to say this is the best team I have ever had. Our objective is to work together to give your mum what she needs so that she can look after you all well. Tomorrow, T and Ali are coming home with us for a sleepover so your mum can really rest. Is everyone up for operation mum?'

Raised hands and a full buy-in. T went straight into issuing tasks and Mandy had a quiet word with Becca and asked her to support T even though they sometimes clashed. By the time dinner was eaten in relative calm, T had each team member on different kitchen duties while Mandy settled Indie with her toys and children's TV.

After half an hour the kitchen was immaculate and Mandy gave T a big hug and thanked her for her hard work. It was past seven now and Dan and Ali asked permission to go and play on their computer games. The other girls chose a film and settled down to watch it and Indie was calm and playing nicely.

At a quarter to eight, a refreshed Naomi came into the living room and looked around amazed at the calm and no mess.

The look on her face was a picture and Mandy just smiled and said, 'Teamwork.'

'You are a fucking genius, pal, I feel a million dollars!' Ni managed.

'It wasn't me; it was this amazing team I found, wasn't it girls?'

'Yes, Mum, we did it because we love you and you needed to sleep,' was T's response and Ni looked stunned.

'Come on, pal, let's get your dinner, all is under control here,' Mandy said, ushering her friend towards the kitchen.

'How the fuck did you manage this? Thank you, you are just...' Naomi's voice was starting to break and Mandy touched her arm and just said, 'We look after each other when we need it, Ni, it works both ways. Now eat because there is a large bottle of Baileys with our name on it.'

Naomi enjoyed her meal uninterrupted and the friends settled for the night with their drinks in hand and a calm house full of happy children.

Chapter 54
December – Boom

After working her last day of the week Mandy had collected her two and two of Ni's girls, two dogs and just managed to make it home. The main road was gritted and passible but dangerous and the farm road had been cleared by tractors, so, despite the weather being relentless, she was still able to get around. The girls enjoyed their sleepover and were as good as gold. Calling Ni to check if she needed any supplies from the shop Mandy set off to take the girls home late Friday afternoon. The stocks in the shop were low so she bought everything Ni needed and extra and topped her own shopping up with as much as she could. Ni looked like a different person today, refreshed, the house was immaculate and she looked rested. Dropping girls and shopping off Mandy stayed for a coffee but then insisted on going home because the snow was getting worse and the forecast was awful.

'We might be snowed in this weekend, Ni, do you have enough of everything?' Mandy asked as she put her coat on and ushered the kids into the car.

'Aye, I'm grand now, pal, take care on the roads, phone me when yae get back so I know you's are OK.'

Mandy agreed to do as Ni asked and headed off to drive in the snow once again. It was almost impossible to see out of the windscreen and it was starting to get dark, what was a five-minute drive took half an hour and when they got back in the house, Mandy vowed that she was not driving again until it was safer. Phoning Ni to tell her how bad it was to drive in the snow she advised her not to leave the house, even on foot unless necessary, this was her safety warning and confirmation of being home. Ni didn't drive but there were no buses running which meant that she was basically trapped with nothing but a tiny village shop. Thank goodness Mandy had picked up extra groceries for her, but with five of them, nothing lasted very long so assuring her friend that she would pick up grocery shopping as soon as the weather improved a bit and, in the daylight, she said goodbye and good luck.

It was two weeks to Christmas and the snow never stopped all weekend. It was impossible to go out in the car and Mandy had to bite the bullet with work and phone all of her clients and tell them it would be January before she was back to work with the weather and the kids being off school.

They were all so understanding, there were no bookings at the holiday cottages anyway and the private clients were in the same situation as her so they just wished her a happy Christmas and said they would see her next year. The downside to being self-employed is that no work means no pay. However, there was no opportunity to spend money so they had to survive on what they had in, there was no petrol being used, so as usual, they would manage.

The logs had been delivered on Monday as had the coal, so the three of them were outside stacking the logs into the shelter and bringing in as many baskets as they could to dry them out in the utility room. The oil delivery had not made it through yet and Mandy was very worried about this because the house was absolutely freezing without the oil heating, just a coal fire was not enough, so she called the oil company daily until there was a positive response. They would be there the day before Christmas eve, it was cutting it tight but it's all they could do.

Only able to get out of the house twice over the next ten days had been really tough. She had to go for shopping and none of the children between her and Ni was old enough to be left home alone, especially in this weather, so she had to drop Becca and Dan off at her friend's house and go and do two major shops at the same time. This had taken her three hours the first time and nearer four the second time as it got closer to Christmas. This left Mandy feeling like she never wanted to shop again, but they were both stocked up and had everything they needed. Unable to stay over at Ni's due to the uncertainty of the weather, Mandy headed home for the last time before Christmas feeling exhausted. The oil delivery was due tomorrow and there was no reading on the dipstick this morning so she was feeling really nervous. They arrived home and unpacked the shopping. The fridge, cupboards and freezer were all full, she could do no more now. Lighting the fire and settling Becca and Dan down while she went off to make the dinner, there was an odd noise. Thinking it was probably just snow falling off the roof she carried on towards the kitchen. It was pizza for dinner because there was no way she was cooking after all of the hours of shopping and driving in the snow, it had depleted her energy. Turning the oven on, a sound bellowed, it was that noise again, it was like grinding metal. Going to check the boiler she instantly noticed the oil gauge. There was no oil left. Quickly turning the boiler off, she bled the air out of the pump and turned everything off. If this delivery didn't turn up tomorrow, they would freeze over Christmas, never mind Christmas, they would freeze tonight!

'Do you not think I have been through enough shit this year?' she said out loud, 'please don't ruin Christmas for me as well, please, Dad, help me out here.'

'Who are you talking to, Mum?' came the voice from the living room.

'Nobody, just talking to myself,' she replied.

This was going to require some rapid action, so heading to the living room to inform the kids that the oil had run out and they had no heating, so they had to have their bath now and then they could eat their pizza in their PJ's. They would need to camp down in the living room because the heating would be off and it would be too cold upstairs. Well, to children this all seems like an adventure, so they were unfazed. It was actually a nice night and they all huddled on sofas and a mattress with the dogs in the living room telling stories until late.

First thing in the morning Mandy was on to the oil company telling them that the oil had run out and if the tanker didn't come today, they would freeze. They promised, but she sat on tenterhooks watching the clock and could think of nothing else. *Stop testing me,* she thought. Eventually, at eleven o'clock, the oil tanker drove past the window and she could have kissed the driver. The tank was filled and the driver helped her to re-boot the system and get the heating back on. Her hands were blue by the time he had gone and she stood at the boiler with her hands on it waiting for the heat to come back. It soon did and within an hour the house was toasty and warm again. Time to set about tidying up and cleaning to get ready for Christmas.

John was calling the kids tonight because as expected he wouldn't make it for Christmas. Dan had been more visibly upset than Becca, but Mandy could see the anger burning beneath the surface with her daughter. To distract them the crafting table had come out and they had made a homemade centrepiece for the Christmas table. John called at around seven and the call lasted about six minutes because he was busy, always too busy with no job? Leaving his children confused, Mandy picked up the pieces as usual.

'It's Christmas eve tomorrow, who's excited?' she asked them.

'Me, me!' they shouted almost simultaneously.

'What do we think Christmas eve breakfast should be then?'

Knowing exactly what the answer would be.

'Pancakes!' came the unanimous response.

'You two are going to turn into pancakes, I have created two pancake monsters!'

They all laughed and decided that tonight's story about Super Jet and Super Ozz should be about saving the town from the pancake monster. Jet ate the pancake monster and he was the town hero.

At least they would be warm in their beds tonight.

'Mum, can I sleep with you and Dan tonight?' asked Becca.

'Of course, you can, sweetie, why don't we watch a film in bed?'

'Yay! Can I pick?' she replied.

'You sure can, but try and pick something you both like, OK?' Mandy urged.

'I will, I know just what to pick, Mum,' Becca replied confidently.

'What's that then?' Mandy asked, already knowing the answer.

'Muppet Christmas Carol,' was the expected response.

'What a great choice, we all love that one, don't we, Dan?'

'Yes, I love tiny Tim,' he replied.

So that was the plan and they stuck to it.

Christmas eve felt good. The heating was on, there was plenty of food, the presents were hidden and Mandy had been able to buy more than was initially planned. Pancakes had been eaten in abundance as usual and the dogs had been on a lovely long walk. It was just coming up to lunchtime and Mandy was thinking about prepping the veg for Christmas dinner when she heard a knock at the door.

Opening the door, she noticed that it was Adam, her landlord.

'Hi, Adam, come in out of the cold. What can I do for you?' Mandy asked.

He entered with a large box.

'I have brought you a Christmas hamper and wondered if I could have a chat with you?' was his response.

'No problem, come in and take a seat, I will just close the living room door so that the kids don't come in,' Mandy said.

She sat opposite Adam at the dining table and waited for him to speak.

'It's actually quite difficult for me, Mandy,' he stuttered, shifting in his seat 'you know that we are Christians?' he asked.

'Yes, I am aware,' was her cautious response, he wasn't going to try and convert her, was he?

'Well, it has been our dream to convert the space at the back of your house and next door into a Christian community. We have the plans signed off and work will start in January. The only issue we have is that we need this house for the Vicar to live in, so it is with much regret that I need to ask you to leave. I am serving you with a Section Twenty-One which gives you until the end of January to move out.'

Mandy took a few seconds to take this news in and then just burst into tears. It was the day before Christmas, it had been an awful year full of the most difficult challenges imaginable, and now she was being made homeless from her beautiful safe haven. This was like a sucker punch to the gut and did not feel very Christian at all. She couldn't speak and just sat and cried while Adam squirmed in his seat.

Chapter 55
December – Christmas

It had taken Mandy several minutes to compose herself. It was the end of a very tough year and this had not been on her radar as even a remote possibility. Adam had felt extremely uncomfortable and not known where to put himself, but once she had composed herself, she thanked him for the hamper and encouraged him out of the door, all the while feeling like kicking him up the backside, but assuring him she would do her best after New Year to try and sort something out.

Anger wasn't a strong enough word to describe how she felt at that moment, not for herself or at anybody in particular, but for her children. They had lost their grandad, their dad and now their home. This was supposed to be her challenge, not theirs, so why the fuck was whoever it was up there setting challenges that were hurting her children? 'Why, Grandad, WHY?' she said out loud. Nobody answered.

Deep breaths, many, many deep breaths. She couldn't let the kids see that she was upset on Christmas Eve, there was no way Christmas would be anything but wonderful for them. She opened the hamper to look at her thirty pieces of silver. This was obviously a softener because it really was a lovely hamper, as she viewed the contents she started to soften and remember that forgiveness and gratitude had to be the bricks and mortar for her to start to rebuild her life. The importance of forgiveness was not lost on her and she knew that everyone had their own agenda and plans that were important to them, after all, she was only a tenant, it was a business transaction, this she could understand.

'Hey, kids, come and look what Adam has brought round for us for Christmas!' she shouted.

The pounding of running feet at the mention of the "C" word.

'What is it, Mum? Let me see.' Becca was already half inside the box searching, 'Oooo chocolates and biscuits and gold coins!' was the muffled noise from inside the box.

Dan was now very interested at the mention of chocolate and they were both pleading to eat the gold coins.

'Well, it is Christmas Eve,' she said.

With that the coins were whisked away to the living room, never to be seen again. When Mandy sorted out the rest of the box there was a huge gammon joint, smoked salmon, jam, marmalade, Christmas cake and pudding, after dinner mints, wine, sherry, port, oatcakes, chocolates, mince pies and you name it. They would eat well this Christmas, she smiled and thought about how hard that must have been for Adam, he was not a bad man, in fact, they had been good to them and had probably spent ages arguing over who would come and tell her. Poor Adam had drawn the short straw. This could be sorted like everything else, but not for a few days, it was Christmas.

Making them all a sandwich for lunch followed by whatever they wanted out of the hamper they enjoyed half an hour in the warmth before going out with the dogs. The weather was still bad, but the driving snow had stopped for now. Many snowballs were thrown, they all returned red-faced and cold so it was lovely to come back into the warm house. Mandy tried not to think about how much she loved this place, it was just a house, they would be happy wherever they were as long as they were together. She needed to think up a story to tell the kids after Christmas where it was her decision to move not forced upon them, they didn't need to be any more upset.

A little voice echoed round the door out of nowhere, 'Why did Dad have to leave, Mum?'

It was Dan, looking really sad.

She scooped him up and tried to explain that sometimes grown-ups don't like each other anymore and that Dad didn't like her so he wanted to live somewhere else, but he still liked them. Dan really didn't understand why anyone would not like her because she was beautiful, but accepted what he was told and went back to his movie.

The rest of Christmas eve was a blur. Managing to prepare everything and sneak presents down happened on autopilot. The kids spoke to both Nana and Grandma but no call from Auntie Angel or their dad. Maybe tomorrow, Mandy had assured them and messaged both of them to make sure that they called on Christmas day.

Christmas was lovely, Becca and Dan loved all of their presents, everybody did call and dinner was the "best dinner ever". But all that Mandy could think about was where were they going to live, how would they afford to move and where would she find both the strength and the words to tell the kids. This was a big challenge indeed, both in terms of mindset and physically. They were completely spoiled with this house and location and she could totally see why Adam and Margaret wanted to create their little slice of heaven here. She knew that they would not be able to afford anything like this again, so it was important that the location was good. But removal costs, carpets etc were not cheap, and there would be a bond to pay and a month upfront for a private let, there was nowhere near enough money for all of that, especially just after Christmas. Unable to borrow anything because she was bankrupt and not wanting to ask her mum, even though she knew that her mum would happily help, but she had her pride and would not ask. Coming up with a way to work this out meant all other plans for her business, networking and self-development would need to be put on hold while this problem was solved, she needed to win, her life depended on it.

Naomi had her mum down for Christmas, so she didn't want to impose on her friend to talk it through, Louise was up to her eyes in it running the pub and finding her own place to live and organise her own move, so she felt so totally and completely alone with this new challenge. Still unable to get out, they were snowed in and going nowhere. Lonely, hurting again and feeling overwhelmed, she messaged Dave, needing to talk to someone.

It was Boxing Day evening when Dave replied and he was amazing. He assured her all would be OK, he had friends that could help and he would make sure that they were looked after. It felt so much better going to bed knowing that she had people in her life that cared so much about her and thanked her lucky stars for good friends.

All of a sudden, she could feel her fight coming back, 'You will not beat me, I will win!'

Chapter 56
January – Mending

The cure for hurt is love. The cure for your own soul is forgiveness and gratitude. There were many people in her life that should have cared and didn't, and there were people in her life that didn't need to care but still did. There had been much time to think over Christmas and New Year and she had sat and considered her options yet again. Looking online at properties to rent it was obvious that there was no way she could afford to take on a private let without having to borrow money. Advice from her friend Dave had directed her to the council, and social housing. Having never lived in a council house before in her life, she had not even considered this as an option. There was still a bit of reservation in her but she needed to get over herself and just do it.

The council offices were closed until the fourth of January so there was a wait, in the meantime, the whole afternoon was spent looking at how she could come up with enough money to move and buy what was needed. There was the bond on this house, then contacting all of her clients to offer them a post-Christmas refresh at a special price and to do some additional decorating at the holiday cottage, all of them had readily agreed.

Another thorough search of the house and a review of her current furniture had identified more items that could be sold as she would definitely be downsizing, her current house was a large farmhouse, so there would be lots of excess things that could generate cash. Acceptance and letting go were the hardest two things to do, but once you managed to get over the initial resistance, it didn't seem so bad. She had decided to sit down and tell the kids on Saturday as they were back to school on Tuesday and the weather was beginning to let up a little.

The three of them had been over to Naomi's and she and her friend had both cried because they would no longer be five minutes away from each other which would make it more difficult, not impossible, but definitely harder to see each other as often. Her mum had been furious with Adam but Mandy had diffused the heat by saying it might be for the best and showing that she had accepted the situation herself.

It was time to tell Becca and Dan and her guts were churning once again.

'I have something to tell you both. Since your dad left, I have been finding it harder and harder to pay the bills here because it is a really expensive house to live in. So, I have decided that I need to find us a smaller house, nearer to shops and things. The snow over Christmas has made this house even more expensive with coal and logs, so we will be moving soon. I am not sure where yet, but I will need you guys to help me to choose a new house.'

'We get to choose?' Becca asked, looking a little upset.

'Yes, we can look at houses and pick the one for us, all of us,' Mandy assured her daughter.

'But who will stroke the cows? And Bob will miss me.'

Becca had named one of the cows, Bob, little did she know they were beef cows and Bob's days were numbered.

'Well, I am sure the cows will miss you but they have each other, just like we have each other and that is what is really important, isn't it?' was the best Mandy could think of.

'Well, yes, I suppose so. Can I decorate my room any way I want to?'

They hadn't been able to do much in this house with it being a private let, but if they had a council house they could do as they pleased, so Mandy saw a win here.

'You can both have your rooms exactly as you choose, that is going to be great fun, isn't it?' she replied hopefully.

'Can I have a Sonic the Hedgehog room?' Dan blurted out excitedly.

'Yes, you can, Son.'

'Yay, when can we move?'

Both of them were unanimous that the room decoration was the win, she had better find more money to buy the paint and paper and be prepared to be creative.

The day they went back to school was a workday so as soon as she was back from her cleaning job, Mandy called the council and informed them of their predicament. To her surprise, because they had been served with a section twenty-one and she was a single parent with a disabled child, they went to the top of the priority list and could bid on houses immediately. The council accepted her application online and unlocked her account so that she could start bidding for properties this week. The new houses to let were released at midnight on a Thursday so it was the first highest priority bidder that was offered the house. Where you lived was dictated by what was available and having driven around some of the estates there was a shortlist of where she did not want to live.

Popping in to see her landlords to let them know what was happening and discussing and exploring options for the oil that had just had delivered, the logs and the coal, none of which she could take with her, they were prepared to speak to the Vicar to see if he was willing to buy them. As they were so amenable, she mentioned the shed that had only been up a year and asked if the Vicar would want to buy that as it was too big to take it with her and they agreed to ask. As she had already paid for all of the fuel and paid monthly for the oil and was up to date if the Vicar bought it all it would be money back in her pocket. The shed had cost two hundred and fifty pounds so she asked for one hundred and twenty-five and hoped for the best. If you don't ask, you don't get, and she was becoming used to having to ask now, it didn't feel quite as uncomfortable as it had done.

There seemed to be a plan coming together and the hurt and anger had dissipated completely. Finding a way to always see a positive in every situation seemed to have become a way of life over the last year, having had to do it so many times. Each time had taught her a new lesson, one that could be used again when needed. There would have been none of these lessons if things had stayed as they were last year, and things were not right as they were, she had not been happy. It was hard to say she was happy now because once again her life was a mixture of problem-solving and solution-seeking, but she was not as unhappy as when John was here and when she was working all of the time. Maybe her soul was beginning to mend properly for the very first time in a very long time. There was definitely hope, but anything other than firefighting, for the time being, was absolutely not on the agenda.

Just fix this, Mandy, and then you might be able to see the path forward, were her thoughts on the way to collect Becca and Dan, ready to set off once again on the dance mum routine.

Chapter 57
January – The Search

It was the end of the first week in January and there had not been any suitable houses in this week's social housing release. There had been houses, but Mandy was just not prepared to compromise on location. If she had to go down this route, then the least she could do was to choose a great location so that her children had somewhere nice to live, they had been spoiled with this house, so it was going to be a tough job to come anywhere near to it. It was like a lottery, but she would not be beaten.

Deciding to ask the universe for what they wanted, she had come up with an activity to do with the kids over the weekend. They were going to drive around her top three choices for location, look at the facilities and then paint a picture together of their perfect house. They were going to manifest it. Despite her hideous challenge, Mandy still believed that if you focused on what you wanted then you could make it happen. The principles were that of the foundations of the book, "The Secret", but also what she knew from her work-life experience. Always blessed with a strong sense of self-worth, thanks to her dad, she had been able to visualise what she wanted and get it with ease in her life before John. Unfortunately, she had allowed him to drag her down to such a negative mindset that it was almost like those skills had been lost to her. Lost but not forgotten, because now she was going to use them to visualise, with her children, exactly where they wanted to live.

The top three choices were, firstly, Felton, which was just a mile from this house and social housing came up only when somebody died, so wishing for a house too hard here felt a bit morbid. Secondly, they had chosen Alnwick, but Mandy really didn't like two of the social housing areas there, but the third was acceptable. Lastly, they had chosen Amble, because it was by the sea and Becca REALLY wanted to live next to the sea. They jumped into the car and set off to the first location, which took a matter of minutes. Driving around the council estates and then the village, there wasn't much there. A small park, a village shop, one pub and a café. Becca didn't like it, Dan thought it was nice because it was not far from his school. Next, they went into Alnwick, they knew it well but had a proper drive around the council estates and Becca hated it, Dan liked it because it was near to the castle and lots of shops and parks. Lastly, they drove to Amble. Mandy didn't know Amble that well, but they had a good drive around and it seemed really nice. Deciding to explore further, they went to the seafront and it was beautiful and stretched for miles. There was a market every Sunday, lots of shops, pubs, café's, chip shops and takeaways and the people seemed really nice. They had a fish and chip lunch in the car because the weather was awful, found an Italian ice cream parlour but it was closed much to their disappointment and as they were driving home, there was a clear favourite.

The painting that was created, mostly by Becca was a house next to the sea, with a chip shop and ice cream parlour nearby. There was no doubting where they wanted to be, but that did not mean that a house would come up there, so Mandy really needed to manage expectations. The main thing was that there was fun had by all and on the dog walk around the triangle even as the snow melted and everywhere was slush, all her children could talk about was living by the sea.

Thursday night came and Mandy was up late, which was hard going because she had worked extra every day this week doing the special cleans and decorating at the holiday cottage. Taking on as many hours as were available doing absolutely anything was leaving her tired, but with a strong sense of purpose, so she was coping admirably. The houses dropped onto the system at midnight so you needed to be poised and ready to make a quick decision and place your bid. Trying not to fall asleep at her laptop Mandy waited, as she waited, she visualised walking on the beach with Becca and Dan and the dogs, knowing they would be happy. She willed there to be a house in Amble, any house, it didn't matter where it was, she could make it nice.

'Please give me a break, Grandad, just a small one,' she asked, but as usual, there was no answer.

The digital clock turned midnight and Mandy refreshed the site and started to scroll through the twenty-eight pages of houses. Feeling a little despondent she was about to click onto page twenty-three when she noticed the very last house at the bottom of page twenty-two. She recognised the house first; they had driven past that very house and there had been a woman loading up a car. It was a nice red brick house the second on the row with a huge front garden. It was there, in Amble, literally seconds from the chip shop and the ice cream parlour as she stared someone placed a bid, quickly clicking to place her bid and kicked herself for not noticing it quicker, it was probably lost now. Clicking through the rest of the pages there were no further houses that were of interest. Deciding not to tell the children in the morning so as not to get their hopes up, she tried to put it out of her mind. Rising from her chair to go to bed her eyes were drawn to Becca's painting and she couldn't believe it, it was the same house, the very same. This was all feeling a bit spooky, it fitted well with her newfound knowledge about manifestation, but having never gone into this much detail before in her life, she had no experience of it. In her career in the past, she had made detailed plans and goals and pinpointed stores to manage and made it happen but that felt more strategic and within her control than this. Or was it?

Heading up to bed she prayed for the first time in a long time that by some divine intervention, something really positive would happen for her. There was doubt though and these challenges had set that doubt in her mind. Anybody would struggle and feel confused if they had been through such a terrible series of events. There were worst things that could happen, so there was much gratitude that her children were healthy despite Dan's potential diagnosis, his physical health was fine, and she had recovered well herself, despite having to take pain medications daily. She was just so desperate to stay alive now, her love for her children had grown, which she didn't think was possible, but the more time that was spent with them the fiercer that love became and the thought of leaving them was her worst nightmare. Searching for answers was driving her insane at times so deciding to just settle her mind and get some sleep she slid into bed and closed her eyes. But sleep didn't come because the answers didn't come. The strain of these challenges was taking its toll and she was worried, really worried, that she had missed her chance of securing their perfect house and in doing so had let her children down.

Chapter 58
January – Kindness

Today was going to be hard work with no sleep, but needs must and the money was welcome. To date, if she included the security bond, she had managed to come up with just under twelve hundred pounds, more than enough to move but not enough for carpets. Her landlords had not come back to her about the fuel or the shed yet so there was hope for more. Thank goodness, it was Friday because rest was needed over the weekend, but tonight was the late night for dance lessons and when she usually did the weekly shopping with Dan while Becca was in classes. Glad that the slow cooker was on from this morning and there would be a hot meal ready when they arrived home, at least that was one less thing to think about.

Dropping Becca off at dance, Mandy wearily went to the supermarket. Dan seemed to pick up on her mood and was playing up much more than usual. They had two hours to kill so Dan was bribed with the promise of a cake in the café if he behaved himself, so he did exactly as he was asked, cake was always a winner with Dan. Managing to fill the full two hours an extra-large black coffee was consumed to keep her awake. Dan had picked the biggest piece of cake in the café and eaten every last crumb, he was a happy boy, Mandy smiled at his cake covered face.

It was dark and wet with melting snow when Becca came out of her dance lesson and the three of them headed back on the ten-mile journey to their current home. Unloading the shopping the smell of the casserole filled their noses and both children ordered extra-large portions. Unpacked and seated to eat within twenty minutes, Mandy thanked the universe for slow cookers.

Halfway through dinner, there was a knock at the door. Telling Becca and Dan to keep eating, Mandy went to answer it. Standing there with a smile on his face was Adam, she greeted him and asked if everything was OK?

'I just stopped by quickly to let you know that the Vicar is really happy to buy the shed and pay you for the fuel and has offered four hundred pounds if that is satisfactory?' Adam said gently.

'That is fantastic, thank him for me, will you?' Mandy replied.

'You can thank him yourself; he has asked if he can come and have a look around the house in the morning? We would also like to offer you some help with your move. I have the big van and two of my lads will be more than happy to load and unload for you, at no charge,' was his kind response and generous offer.

'I don't know what to say, thank you so much, Adam, this means a lot,' Mandy managed, trying hard not to let the tears well up in her eyes, but feeling really emotional, 'and of course, the Vicar can come around in the morning, we leave for dance lessons at ten thirty so around nine-thirty would be best.'

'That is perfect, do you have any news on a house or a date for moving yet?'

'Not yet, but I put a bid in on a house on Thursday, so your prayers would be appreciated,' was the only thing Mandy could think of to say.

'Of course, I will let you get back to your dinner, thank you, Mandy, you have been a lovely tenant and I am genuinely sorry about this,' Adam offered and seemed really authentic.

'I know, it will be for the best and right for you.'

It was time for her to truly let go of any remaining anger and absolve these kind people.

As she re-joined her children at the dinner table, she wondered how long it would take the council to let her know about the house she had bid on. Suspecting it would not happen until bidding closed on Tuesday she decided to just try and put it out of her mind and get on with her usual routine, the second guessing could drive you around the bend. Hope was the only card she had to play now, this situation would be whatever the powers that be dictated, and if there were to be further challenges ahead then she had no choice but to rise to them and prevail.

Chapter 59
January – Worthless

The weekend had been quiet as a result of the melting snow and residual water, which severely restricted any sort of outdoor activity. It was wet dogs and wet towels all weekend. Becca's painting of their house by the sea had kept its prime position on the dining room wall and they had talked about living by the seaside all weekend. The Vicar had been lovely and so apologetic about making them homeless, but once again Mandy had absolved him of any guilt by telling him it was for the best.

Monday loomed with a full extra day of painting at the cottage, but it was one hundred and twenty pounds worth of work and there were no after school classes on a Monday so Mandy had just scheduled it in and thought about the reward.

Picking the kids up covered in paint, she caught up with Ni and promised to go for coffee in the morning before her cleaning job to catch up. Everything felt a bit flat and the minutes seemed to be clicking by at half speed because she was waiting to hear about the house. As they pulled up at home her phone rang and she did not recognise the number, answering it any way she said, 'Hello.'

'Is this Mrs King, I am speaking to?' the caller asked.

'Yes, it is, how can I help and can I ask who I am speaking to?' was her quizzical reply.

'It is Jeanette Holmes from the council here, I am calling about the house in Amble that you placed a bid on last week. I am pleased to inform you that we will be offering the house to you and closing the bidding. You should receive a letter to confirm this in the morning.'

Tears pricked Mandy's eyes, they were tears of relief that she had found a home for her children and that their manifesting had actually worked.

'Thank you so much, Jeanette, you just made my day, thank you,' Mandy replied.

'You are welcome, Mrs King; I hope that you will be happy in your new home.'

The call ended and it was time to tell Becca and Dan that they were moving into the house that they had painted.

To say that they were excited was the understatement of the year, jumping up and down and singing, "We are living by the seaside, we are living by the seaside," on a continuous loop made Mandy smile and her heart feel full. What had looked like another awful challenge and had broken her heart on Christmas eve, had resulted in a silver lining. It was still an adjustment for Mandy however, in her thinking, she did see this as a monumental fall from grace. It was not that long ago that she was a senior leader on a six-figure salary and now she was going to be a cleaner living in a council house with nothing other than her little car and loose change in her bank account. This felt like she had now hit rock bottom, even though the solution to the latest challenge was a positive one, in her mind, it felt like her place was at the bottom of society. Nothing, she had absolutely nothing other than her house contents, her car, her children and pets. Knowing that there were worse things that could still happen did not console her in her mindset of lack. She actually felt worthless.

Having never experienced this feeling before, it was a stranger to her. *Worthlessness was really low,* she wondered. Is this how her friend Naomi felt when she was low? She decided to call her friend and ask the question.

'Hey, pal, how're things? Firstly, we got the house so we will be moving to Amble and secondly I wanted to ask you a question.'

Ni was the only person that it was comfortable being this open and honest with.

'Hi, lovely, that's fantastic and nae bother ask away,' her friend responded in her usual warm and caring way.

'I feel really weird. Like I am no longer worth anything, and I don't mean money-wise, I mean like I just am nothing. I am just a cleaner about to move into social housing and I have nothing. I feel worthless, and that is odd to me because I have always had such a positive view of myself. I don't know what to do.'

'Ahh, pal, I understand that feeling better than anyone. I wake up every day feeling worthless, I tell myself I am a bad mother because of T and the fact I had all of that money and spent it on things. I feel like I am not worth anybody caring about. Some days I can't even face living, that is why I am on so many anti-depressants. Maybe ye need to go and see the doctor, just to get ye through this. It's been one hell of a year; I don't even know how ye get through the day with all that has happened. But ye are the most amazing woman I know and worth so much more than the shit ye have had thrown at ye. Try not to let it take ye down, pal, it is not a nice place to be, take it from someone that lives in that dark place every day.'

Ni's response stopped her in her tracks. Knowing that someone suffers like her friend did and feeling it was two different things, maybe she did need some help. Having used food as her comfort, like always, and gained so much weight in this year, her body image was at an all-time low. The drugs prescribed for her pain didn't help, but her self-esteem was non-existent and her thinking was negative. These challenges had taken their toll on her ability to pick herself up and brush herself off. She was still solving the problems and rising to the challenges, but in using up her strength being in constant fight or flight mode, it had somehow drained her of herself and sucked out her confidence. Maybe this place of mental confusion was actually her next challenge. Knowing that she needed to face this for the sake of her children made things worse, at this very moment, all that was on her mind was giving in, and the need for a damn good cry.

Answering her friend and trying hard to pull herself around she managed, 'Ni, I think you are right; I need help, I think I will make an appointment at the doctors' tomorrow. Thanks, pal, love you.'

Ending the call, she promised to go for coffee in the morning and talk again.

Knowing something and doing it are two different things. Mandy knew that comfort eating was not the answer, but with no other bad habits like drinking or smoking, what else was she supposed to do when she felt like this. Eating dinner with the kids and then eating again when they were in bed, stuffing her face with biscuits and chocolate, Mandy felt like a slug. But she couldn't stop herself, this was the lowest feeling on earth. Worthless. Why would this feeling not go away?

Going to bed full of carbohydrates was uncomfortable, it underlined the need for some help. Vowing to call the doctor first thing and go and talk about things, she tried to sleep. But the dark place had other ideas. You are not good enough. You were never good enough; it was all a lie. It was luck, not talent, you are really just an imposter. You will never be anything again. Nobody will love you, why would they, you are fat.

The voices just kept coming, all night. No sleep.

In the morning as she smiled and hugged her children, Becca gave her an extra big hug and said, 'What is wrong, Mum? You have sad eyes.'

Was it that bad that it was visible? It must be, she had to get help for her own sake and for the sake of her family. She had responsibilities. Feeling desperate Mandy picked up the phone and called the doctors and asked for an emergency appointment and managed to get one for during dance and karate classes when she had no children.

Becca held her hand all the way to the school bus and gave her the biggest hug and parted for school with the words, 'Don't be sad, Mum, we love you and you are the best mum in the whole wide world. I hope I grow up to be just like you.'

As her daughter boarded the school bus the tears stung her eyes and she headed for coffee and talk with her friend, feeling very low but very lucky at the same time.

Chapter 60
January – Becca

The doctor had been really empathic and just talking to him, and crying had helped her to re-frame her thinking. No medication at this point she had decided, taking so much pain medication, the drug cocktail did not need any additions. At home, it was time to sit and consider how she was describing herself and why? How could she forget all of the positive and successful things in her past and only focus on the negatives, that had never happened before? Sitting with her journal and pen it was time to keep a record of how her feelings were on a daily basis and make an active attempt to find an alternative from what was negative. Knowing so much about the theory, why was this feeling so difficult? She felt weighed down with everything that had happened. Grief, worry, loss, hurt and disappointment had been the constants in her life for almost a year now; in order to survive and thrive there had to be alternative thoughts that would replace them. This would be her task in the coming weeks because there was so much to juggle with moving.

Oh, my Lord, Becca's birthday! the thought just popped into her head.

It was her daughter's birthday in just a few days and she would need to use some of the moving budget to buy her a present. This little girl was the most wonderful gift ever received in her entire life, not only because she was a bit of a miracle after the ectopic pregnancy, but because of her individuality. Walking at ten months and climbing by the age of one, Mandy had always known they had been blessed with a feisty one. Becca had taught herself how to use the potty by watching a potty-training video over and over and copying. Her favourite films had been Jurassic Park and Deep Blue Sea, dinosaurs and sharks at age two! Crashing around the house in her walker Mandy had constant bruises on her legs from her one hundred miles an hour baby. Talking by eighteen months, climbing into and onto everything, removing every ornament, book and video in everybody's house, she was a terror, but the cutest most loveable terror ever. Breastfed until age two, her first word had been, "Booby," mostly in the supermarket or another public place.

They had taken her to Disney World in Florida at two and a half and she had dived in at the deep end of the pool with her water wings on shouting, "Bombs Away," and given them all heart failure. But there were the tough parts as well because her first Christmas was spent in Lincoln hospital after being rushed in blue lighted, having had a febrile fit, only for them to discover that she had a kidney condition that was causing nasty infections. She spent her entire childhood taking antibiotic after antibiotic, becoming immune, getting sick then trying a new one. But you would never guess that she was sick because she was so full of fun and Mandy had become an expert at spotting the signs and taking rapid action.

The smartest, most outspoken and rebellious in her class, her teachers had both loved her and rolled their eyes at her daily. At age five she had sauntered into class and exclaimed, "Hello, good morning and how are your bollocks?" because she had been nosing while her dad had watched a grown-up cartoon. Mandy had been called in to see the teacher for that one and didn't know whether to apologise or laugh.

Funny, clever and the life and soul of any party, Becca Louise was a beautiful gift and precious addition to their lives. How her dad could ever leave her, Mandy would never understand until the day she died.

Thinking about her daughter had really lifted her mood, and if that little girl could be so happy then there was no excuse for her mood being low. There was a lesson here and it was noted and acknowledged. What Mandy did not know yet was that the brave face her daughter was currently demonstrating at age nine, was a shield for some terrible things that had happened whilst in her dad's care, but this would not reveal itself for ten more years and would initially show up as anger, anxiety and depression that nobody would understand, until Becca found the words to share.

For now, she was her mum's biggest inspiration and would be the shining light that would carry her back from the darkness.

Decision made, there would be no expense spared for Becca's birthday, she could have whatever her heart desired. With a smile on her face and feeling stronger, Mandy set off on the school and dance runs as was her lot in life. And what woman wouldn't be proud as punch to have the honour of being called mother by these two angels? Life was not that bad and she would find strength in every thought and fight the darkness like a Goddess. Nobody was going to take her down.

Chapter 61
January – Moving

Becca had purposely chosen a very meagre present for her birthday. How had she known at nine years old that her mum was struggling? Mandy would probably never know, but that is what she did. Deciding to become vegetarian because of Bob the cow and asking to sponsor a tiger, her little girl was finding her moral compass and making big decisions all by herself. They had gone out to eat at a vegetarian restaurant and all enjoyed it and that had made Becca's day.

Thoughts of moving were at the forefront of Mandy's focus and it was going to be hard work to pack up while working all the extra hours, but she would find a way. The additional work had generated over seven hundred pounds, there was the money for the fuel and shed, selling excess furniture and more items online had managed another four hundred and with no removal fees to pay there was enough for the whole house to be carpeted and the kid's bedrooms to be decorated how they wanted. This meant that her promise to them could be kept and that made her feel good.

Checking on Freecycle for packing boxes, Mandy had been lucky to find some not too far away and her friend Dave had picked them up and come to help her pack up. When he had arrived, Mandy had butterflies in her stomach and felt cared about once again, but was not allowing anything but her head to rule her life from now on, so they would remain friends. Dave wanted more and that was obvious, but he was in a long-term relationship and Mandy was not prepared to be that person even though she cared about him deeply. "No complications," she resolved, the pecking order was her first, because she had to look after everyone else, then the kids and then the dogs, so there was no room at the Inn.

The house didn't take as long as she had imagined to pack up but there would be a need to paint a couple of rooms to leave them in pristine condition, she would exit the house with pride, leaving it immaculate. Planning this into her diary she had called the council for a moving date and all was agreed for the fourth of February, exactly eleven months since her car crash and her challenge had been set.

So much had happened, sometimes she couldn't even fathom how much. There had been losing her job, Dan's diagnosis, losing her dad, the pub, the debt, the bankruptcy, the awful issues with her sister and their relationship, the breakdown of her marriage, John's complete abandonment of his children, the poverty, the snow and now the loss of her beloved home and having to start a new life in a strange place. All of this while still trying to recover from her physical injuries and hold down enough work to pay the bills had finally taken its toll on her mental health, but she was a fighter and would never be beaten on any challenge. The skills and knowledge that she had amassed over her lifetime would now be her tools to move her onwards and upwards and maybe, just maybe this move was a beginning and not an end.

She liked that. A new beginning, that is how she was going to think and write this in her journal from now on. It would take some focus, but just deciding to do it was the first step. Taking the first step in any journey was always the hardest, she had done harder things.

With most of the house packed and some of the painting complete over the weekend, Mandy headed to the big house to speak to Adam and Margaret about her moving date, the van and help they had promised. They were both very nice to her and had been more than accommodating with the help they offered. The van would come and collect the first load at 8 a.m. on the fourth while Mandy did the school run and drove to Amble to meet the council, pick up the keys and let the carpet fitters in, Adam's men would load the van and be over at the new house for lunchtime. The carpet fitters had promised it would only take a couple of hours to lay all of the flooring and carpets, the house was only half the size of her current one so she thought that was probably accurate.

Ni had agreed to pick up the kids from school and give them their tea so Mandy could get their beds made up and rooms ready. Her mum was coming to help unpack and hoover so that it could be turned around quickly, everything was organised and planned in the greatest detail with the children in mind. The move itself was upheaval enough for them, the least she could do is make it feel seamless so that they could settle in immediately. Decorating bedrooms would come at the weekend after the move, so, all in all, it wouldn't take long and Mandy was confident. Planning everything had given her a stronger sense of

200

purpose and eased her depression considerably. Meeting this challenge head-on just like she had done with every other event as it had cropped up was actually a big achievement. It was about time that she started giving herself some credit for all that had been achieved, that is where she had fallen down because being so busy in fight or flight mode, she had neglected to speak kindly to herself and give herself some praise. That was going to change. With so much work still to do on her mindset, this seemed like a positive step in the right direction. Things were evening off, a little.

Chapter 62
February – Settling

It was just before seven in the evening when Mandy arrived at Ni's to collect her children on moving day, she was exhausted but at the same time pumped up on adrenaline. The house looked lovely, small, but lovely. She and her mum had managed to get everything unpacked, everywhere cleaned and the kid's bedrooms perfect including a little welcome gift for each of them. The dogs were happy in their new doughnut beds in the dining room and it had been a real accomplishment.

'How was the move, pal?' Ni asked as Mandy made her way into the hallway.

'It went like a dream. I was waiting for a disaster but it all went to plan; I am actually still amazed and expecting something to blow up!' she chuckled.

Ni laughed and said, 'Now that is the Mandy I know and love, it's nice to see your spark back again.'

'You're right, Ni, I have been searching, but it has been one step forward and ten back all year, maybe now I can start on a blank page and write a new story.'

'I know ye can, pal, I have never met anyone with your strength, ye will bounce back higher and all of the bastards that have hurt ye can watch you rise, like a fucking phoenix.'

Her friend hugged her tighter than ever, knowing that they would see each other so much less frequently now.

'Come on, you two,' Mandy shouted, 'we have a new house to explore and the dogs will be making the most of being on their own and lounging on the sofas.'

The thunder of two pairs of feet followed and lots of happy squealing noises. They were so excited to explore their new environment, but it was too dark now so Mandy would need to manage expectations and make some plans for after school tomorrow in order to keep them both happy. Bidding her friend an emotional goodbye and making her promise to come over at the weekend the three of them set off for their new home, and they would spend their first night ever in social housing. Mandy knew she should feel lucky, and she did on one hand, but there was still this feeling of failure on the other and the two were fighting and tearing her logic apart.

Pulling up in her reliable little car outside her new house Becca and Dan were running up the path before she had even silenced the engine.

'Hold on, you two, you can't get in until I open the door.'

'But, Mum, hurry up, we are excited!' Becca replied unable to contain herself.

Opening the door, children spilling into the hallway and being greeted by two very bouncy dogs, it all felt very surreal, almost like she hadn't been here before, despite spending the whole day creating the theatre for their arrival. There was much oohing and aahing as her children looked in the downstairs rooms, even checking out the substantial back garden.

'I love it, Mum, it feels so cosy, and the dogs have new beds!' Becca said and then shot upstairs to see her room with Dan following on her heels. 'Mum, this is amazing!' was the shout down the stairs as Becca discovered her gift.

Mandy had bought her daughter some new PJ's, slippers and a dressing gown to wear in her new house and the same for Dan with Sonic the Hedgehog on them. They both had new bedding, throws, bins and bedside lights so everything was set up to feel like it was special. The children had picked their carpet colours and Dan had gone for Sonic the Hedgehog blue and Becca for purple, so their rooms already had their stamp on them, Mandy just needed to paper one wall and paint the others in each room and they would be completely individual, and a perfect family activity for the weekend.

'Right, bath time, and I think we could have a sneaky movie downstairs before bed tonight, even though it's a school night,' she offered as a treat to keep her children feeling upbeat.

'This is the best day ever, Mum,' Becca said, 'I love our new house, when can we go to the beach?'

'Well, you can either get up at 6 a.m. with me in the morning when I walk the dogs or we can go after school and dance tomorrow night?' she replied.

'Both, please, Mum,' was Becca's unexpected reply.

'What about you, Dan?'

'Both, Mum,' assured Dan.

They were ready to explore and if they wanted to get up at six then who was she to disagree with them?

'Well, that's a deal then, all five of us are going to explore the beach in the morning, it will be dark mind, we will need torches,' she warned.

'That makes it even better, Mum,' replied Becca, not to be beaten.

With that, Mandy hoped it didn't rain overnight or in the morning and went to run them their first bath in the new house. Once clean and both dressed in new bedtime kit, they all went downstairs to watch a movie with supper of their choice and hot chocolate. Tucking them both in bed just before ten and telling them a new Super Jet and Super Ozz story, where they all saved Amble from a rouge shark, Mandy wearily walked the dogs and slid into her own bed tired to the bones but happy that she had managed to pull this off in the right way for Becca and Dan. This was now her world and there was no choice but to make the best of it if she was going to rise as high as Ni had indicated. Blank page.

The alarm went off at six and to her surprise, Becca was up and dressed before her, she popped her head around Dan's door and his eyes shot open and he jumped out of bed. It wasn't raining but it was cold and dark, so they all wrapped up warm, put their wellies on and set off with dogs and torches towards the beach. It was literally a left turn, a short walk and a road to cross and they were on a huge green area before the sand dunes, sixty seconds from the house. The dogs could run free and they walked for a good thirty minutes on the beach and sand dunes in the dark, listening to the lapping of the waves against the shore. It was a calm that Mandy had not experienced before, the sounds of the sea at this time of the day were soothing and reassuring. It was hard work dragging all four of the excited family members back home, everybody just wanted to stay out, the dark and the cold not even noticed because they were having too much fun.

Back at the house a hearty breakfast and the benefits of gas central heating brought up rosy cheeks and cosy feet, but the smiles were directly from the heart.

Not a bad start to the day, Mandy thought to herself. The school run was now eight miles instead of one so they had to leave the house on the dot of eight so that Becca could make her bus connection, but being such early birds today, this was not a problem. With Dan dropped off at breakfast club for eight-thirty, Mandy was back in the house at quarter to nine and had a full hour before she needed to leave for her first job, so there would be plenty of time to do housework with this routine, keeping on top of it daily so that she never got behind. After work it was possible to be home, walk the dogs and still be back at school in time for pick up, it just meant a little more driving and would cost an extra eighty pounds a month for petrol, but there was now going to be saving of more than three hundred on rent and utilities, so she was still considerably better off. This could actually be a turning point for her and she decided it was time to look at her goals and set some new ones. Blank page.

Chapter 63
February – Forgiveness

Getting into a new routine had been easy, not that the kids wanted to get up at six every morning, the novelty of that had worn off after a couple of days. They had explored more of the area after school and been down to the beach whilst it was light. There were actually four separate beaches one after the other, each one bigger than the previous one, so Mandy was able to plan the dog walks for poor weather and for fair weather according to beach size, not a bad problem to have. Ozzy had discovered a new love, chasing seagulls and he would run for miles trying to catch them as they were flying past while Jet plodged in the sea with the kids.

This place was a tonic. It is like the sea air had completely cleared her mind and reset it to positive. Coming home from the school run with no job to go to, Mandy set about creating her new goals for her fresh start. She had read a great little book recently called, "The Game of Life" and "How to Play It" which had resonated so much because of her challenge, as soon as she had seen the title. It had been written in the 1920s by a really enlightened artist and illustrator called Florence Scovel Shinn and in it, she had described life as a perfect square consisting of health, wealth, love and self-expression. This was where Mandy had decided to start by setting one goal in each area and see how it felt for her.

Sitting down at her desk with a blank piece of paper and a pen, excited and full of expectations about what would appear on the paper, after thirty minutes there was nothing. Why were no ideas coming? Closing her eyes and trying to clear her mind the same thought kept repeating itself. How can you create goals that you believe in if you are still feeling angry and like a failure?

What was it that was making her feel like this? The house was great, the location was amazing and the kids were happy. What was eating at her? Deciding to just write anything, the first thing that came into her head she let the pen make a mark on the paper and just stopped trying too hard.

Forgive yourself.

'Did I just write that?' she puzzled.

Forgive others. Forgive.

The word kept appearing on the page like it was being written by somebody else. She laid down her pen and studied the words.

Had she really forgiven everyone that had done her harm? How did she really feel? Deciding to write down everything that had happened and how she felt about it, how she really felt, no holds barred, she placed her pen on the paper once again.

The crash and the challenge – happy at the second chance but angry at the amount that had been thrown at her.

Losing her job – bloody angry, she was good at it.

Dan's diagnosis – angry at John and his mother for not believing it or supporting her.

Her sister and the pub – bloody angry at her sister's stupidity and for not asking for help and even more angry at herself for not seeing it.

Dad's death – bloody angry at God and her grandad for this nasty trick. Angry at Amy for her pathetic behaviour.

The end of her marriage – not bothered but angry at John for abandoning the kids.

Being made homeless – angry because it wasn't very Christian and felt unaligned with her own values.

Being poor and living in a council house – angry and ashamed because she had failed.

Bloody hell, she thought, *look at all that anger that was still there,* no wonder she couldn't move forward. Recognising that there was some work needed on this, there would be no movement from this seat until she had worked through each one and come up with a reason to disperse the anger. Back to the start, blank page.

The challenges – they were a gift in order to give her a second chance, she had asked for it and been up for it so what was there to be angry about? She had learned a lot; done things she would never have done. Grateful.

Losing her job – this had allowed her to be there for her dad. Not entirely happy and definitely overworked. This was a gift and had pushed her into thinking and learning new skills. She had started her own business! Grateful.

Dan's diagnosis – John had not been present when they were still together so why would this behaviour be anything that she shouldn't expect? She had to learn to accept that not everyone was like her and that he may have his own demons that he was dealing with. She had Dan and Becca with her and she was a great mum. Grateful.

Her sister and the pub – Angel was struggling big time. What her sister had done was what she had been allowed to do all of her life, unchecked and definitely enabled by her and her mum and dad. Angel could not think of anyone else because of where her depression had taken her, it was a selfish disease. It was Mandy's duty to be there when she came out the other side. The rest was only money and money was made and lost all of the time. She still had her sister so there was still hope. Grateful.

Her dad's death – when she thought about this it was clearly something that may have been inevitable due to his trauma when he broke his neck. Why would you be angry at anybody for that? Amy was irrelevant and removed from her life which was a relief. It had been lucky to be able to see her dad as often as she had before he died. Grateful.

Her marriage breakdown – this was a real gift having been so unhappy with John. She had no control over how he behaved towards his children so she needed to let it go, his loss was her gain. Grateful.

Being made homeless, living in social housing – her landlords had to do what was right for them, it was their right to do it, not personal. The amount of money she could now invest in savings for her children was considerable, this was the biggest benefit. A house was a house. Grateful.

Now that looked like a much better viewpoint and the act of writing it all down had been a weight lifted. Deciding to practice this level of forgiveness and gratitude morning and night for the next couple of weeks before trying to create any new goals, she felt at peace.

Chapter 64
February – Mindset

The daily act of practising forgiveness and gratitude, along with the sea air and the lower costs were all helping Mandy to feel a lot more positive. It felt like forgiveness and gratitude were the bricks and mortar for her to start to rebuild her life. If you practice new thought processes daily, they begin to form new pathways in your thinking, it was the repetition that was starting to work and the way that she was beginning to talk to herself.

Still being cautious and taking her time, Mandy began to add positive affirmations to the mix. Having studied coaching and achieved four diplomas, she knew the theory, so it was time to put it into practice.

Coach, coach thyself!

The connection between practising forgiveness and gratitude and her own mindset began to become really clear, almost like the shift in mindset was like adding the windows to the re-build. Visibility was improved and it was easier to stop viewing things in such a negative way. Starting to describe her little council house as her "Castle by the Sea," it changed how it looked in her mind. The reduction in her outgoings was a massive opportunity to live small and plan big, investing in herself, her business and her children's future.

Your mindset and the difference it made to your life was immensely powerful and felt like an ever-moving concept. Seeing the world in colour and pictures as a natural state had become alien after working in such a left-brained industry. Having stood out in that environment when she had used her creative thinking, it had been a great lesson that wasn't being used to its full effect right now. Deciding to help to release her mind with some meditation, she was trying hard to repair her thinking so that her best asset could be leveraged in order to get her back on track. All of these new practices were working, but she was under no illusions about the time and effort that would need to be invested in order to make more permanent changes in her mindset. Most importantly, there was some light at the end of this particular tunnel and she was winning in breaking the negative patterns that had been going on in her head. Longer walks and less time thinking negatively had resulted in a change to her fitness and eating patterns so she felt healthier in mind and body. What had been something that had made her feel ashamed, was actually turning out to be the biggest gift of all. Who would have guessed that so much gratitude could be found after so much loss and hurt, but it was possible?

Realising what was possible opened up even more space for thinking that anything was possible and day by day she could feel the old Mandy returning. The one that was confident and decisive and saw opportunities in every single problem, just like when she was a store manager. Maybe there was something in that too, that was worthy of some additional thought.

Chapter 65
February – Skills

As a manager, there had never been a moment in the day where she had not been problem-solving. Initially doing it herself and then coaching her team on how to do it for themselves, she eventually made herself redundant. To her, this had been a huge positive and usually the moment when she reached the point where her team did not need her, was the time she had been promoted. There was no longer a team as such, but she really did think hard about the principles and how they could be applied to life. How would she develop her team, who were they, what benefit would this have for them and for her? So many questions and this was great because it meant that her creative and inquisitive thinking was starting to return and she was thinking big. This is where the start line was in order to create a better life and rise.

Thinking about her initial problems that needed solutions, her children came to mind. They really needed stability and support, Dan, with his autism and how he fitted into the world and Becca with her anger at her dad. Mandy recognised that she may need to learn more in order to help them both and her mind flicked immediately to the Open University degree, this was an opportunity to learn a lot so she decided to explore this fully in the next few days.

Doing just that and discovering that as a single mum on a low income supported by benefits, she would automatically qualify for a fully funded degree course, this lifted her to a new level. Meeting all of the entry criteria with so many previous qualifications, and identifying that part of the program was child psychology, it was perfect. The first module started in March so if she completed all of the paperwork and submitted her application immediately, then they would try and get her onto that course, it was called, "You and Your Finances" which seemed a pretty good place to start.

Feeling alive again in taking this action it was like she was worthy, good enough and that was a great feeling. So maybe this was not just to help her children, it was also to help her. It didn't matter how this degree was used, what mattered was how it made her feel and what was actually learned. This was about doing what she loved, always a lifelong learner and never wanting to stop, this was the real Mandy, the one who wanted to know the theory and the practice, the one who sought answers and solutions to problems. She would never be an academic, always an entrepreneur and a bit artsy and hippy-like prepared to take risks, to make mistakes and to go for everything big style. These traits had served her well in the past in her business life, so they would continue to do so if she allowed them back in.

Just because she felt like she had hit rock bottom a few short weeks ago, did not mean that staying there was an option, it might take her some time, but she was ready to start, ready to play the game of life and win.

I am ready, world, bring on the new challenges, I will find the solutions because I know how to ask for help.

Chapter 66
March – Coastline

As February clicked into March the weather was actually starting to improve and Mandy and her pack were ready to do some more exploration. They had fully investigated beaches one and two which were closest to the house on a daily basis and they were ready to go further afield. It was Saturday and dance lessons were finished, lunch was eaten and they were getting ready to head to beach three and maybe even number four. The weather was fine, they were kitted out in walking boots and had bottles of water, the dogs were ready and off they went.

'I have decided, Mum, that we should aim to buy a bigger house one day,' Becca piped up, as they exited the estate and passed the posh houses along the seafront.

'I totally agree, Becca, and your mum is working on that, but you know that houses cost a lot of money and that it might take a long time,' was her slightly amused reply.

Children had such a simple view of the world; it was her responsibility to teach them the value of material things and how to think about them.

'How much would that house cost, Mum?' Becca responded pointing to a lovely big bungalow adjacent to the dunes.

'I would guess that the house would cost about three hundred thousand pounds, Becca.'

'Whoa, really! How long would that take to save up, Mum?'

'Give me ten years, Becca, and we will live in an even better house than that. It takes time, but remember how we manifested the house we live in now; I think we should draw our perfect house and leave it to the universe to deliver it, what do you think?'

She really wanted her daughter to understand that it was OK to have big goals and that she could achieve them, how she reacted needed to be consistent. Never would the words we can't or that is out of our reach leave her lips, she vowed to always speak to her children as if everything was achievable, but to also manage their expectations.

They walked past beach two and carried on towards the next beach, over the dunes, past the white house on the hill and as they reached the path to the beach the sun shone and both of her children and both of her dogs started to run towards the vast, beautiful space that lay at the end of the path. Mandy caught up and watched them run, it was stunning. White sand striped with intermittent rows of fine pebbles. The sea was sapphire blue, morphing into turquoise with white foamy tips lapping the sand. They were the only ones there, it felt like the rest of the world was missing out on this hidden secret, and she was glad because at this moment she wanted it all to herself. Catching up with her delirious children who looked like they had entered wonderland, they were laughing at Jet who was already in the sea and running in and out like people do when the water is too cold. Ozzy was in his element and chasing seagulls up the coastline, it really looked like he had a smile on his face. Becca found a piece of driftwood and was throwing it into the sea for Jet to retrieve which he was doing with no arguments and Dan was drawing Sonic the Hedgehog in the sand with another stick. It was a scene of unabandoned happiness and Mandy just took it all in.

'Can I go into the sea with Jet?' Becca asked.

'Absolutely not, believe me, Becca, it's March and that is the North Sea, it will be freezing and we did not come prepared for that. In a few weeks when the weather gets warmer you can go in, but not today. Why don't you collect pebbles and shells and we can make something when we get home?' she offered as a consolation, not knowing at this stage that Becca would be in the sea at every single opportunity during their time there, she had always been a water baby.

'OK, come on, Dan lets go and find the best pebbles and shells on the beach. Look, Mum, there are rock pools over there, will there be crabs?'

'Why don't you go and find out, but be careful you don't slip in and keep an eye on Dan.'

And off they ran towards the rock pools, with her and Jet trying hard to keep up. Ozzy was just a dot in the distance one minute and then back with them the next as he picked his seagull to chase and followed its flight path.

They spent three hours on beach three that day. Not one of them wanted to go home, but Mandy had to insist as it neared five o'clock as she could feel the cooler air and knew the light would start to go soon. With the promise of fish and chips when they got back, she managed to convince them and they set off on the trek home carrying a large number of rocks and shells that would be converted into works of art tomorrow. As they walked, the joy of that first visit to that particular beach embedded itself in her memory with the visuals, the sounds and the smells all playing their own role in anchoring it there. The happiness that she felt at this moment needed to be bottled and sold because it was such an empowering and positive feeling. Deciding to use the feelings that she currently had to drive her actions in the next few hours and days, plans began evolving, the biggest one was the perfect house, she would start there.

It was one of the best meals they had eaten in ages, whether that was the appetite they had worked up or just great fish and chips, she didn't care, it had been so good they were all feeling full and content. An even bigger bonus was no washing up, so clearing the paper and packets away Mandy left her children deciding which were the best pebbles and shells while watching a film. Opening her journal, she started to capture the emotions from the day and think about how to recreate them as the norm in their lives. Happiness was the absolute best tonic in the world, so the ultimate goal was to ensure that they were all happy. Drawing a square and labelling each side she started to think about what was important in each area and just write words down under each heading. Wealth, health, love and self-expression for her and for each of her children. This would actually be a great activity for them all to do tomorrow, but for now, she continued writing down her words and thoughts.

In the centre of the square, she had written HAPPINESS and decided to connect anything that was set as a goal in each of the four areas of life with that word. From today forward she was not going to do anything that did not make her and her children happy.

On Sunday Becca and Dan were excited to have a day of creating their vision boards and rock and shell masterpieces. They all made the square into their perfect house and they were encouraged to describe everything they wanted in their house. When they had completed the activity, the house was crystal clear; it would have four big bedrooms, three bathrooms, a huge kitchen-diner with a family area, a big living room and a separate garage and utility, with large gardens front and rear for all the dogs Becca wanted. Mandy would turn the fourth bedroom into an art studio and she would be creating art for a living. They would be happy and comfortably off and eat in all the posh vegetarian restaurants all the time, again, according to Becca. Mandy had written a great big ten on hers and told her children that she would need time to make this happen but they all needed to believe that they could have it. To her surprise she was not a single mum anymore and had described her perfect man in the love section, he was not imminent but he was there and he would be different and the choice would be made with her head and her heart this time. Under wealth, all that Mandy had written was, "build a successful business and invest in three things as it grows: me, the business and the children's future". Not able to see anything more specific than that at this time, she let it sit there and knew it would come. The self-expression part was the hardest because of her desire to get back to creating art, but having lost her confidence a little she was not sure that she would be good enough after all this time. For now, she would focus on creative thinking, educating herself and encouraging the kid's creativity.

All in all, it had been a really fun and productive day and feeling accomplished they were all in bed by nine-thirty ready for the new school week.

Chapter 67
Fourth of March 2010 – Possibilities

It was her day off and returning from the school run Mandy noticed the date, exactly one year from the day of her crash. It had been around six weeks since her last big challenge, being made homeless, and yet here she was, settled in her little, "Castle-by-the-sea" and feeling really happy for the first time in a long time. Drinking her after school coffee in the dining room, she reviewed the vision boards and the rock and shell art from the previous day and smiled. Knowing there was a long way to go no longer felt like a problem, there was a journey to be embarked upon here, of that she had no doubts, but for some reason that eluded her, it felt like her mindset and universe had shifted. Deciding to do the housework and then go to beach four with the dogs alone to assess how far it was for little legs, she made a move.

By eleven with the house clean, the ironing completed, dinner prepped in the slow cooker and switched it on, she had a snack and pulled on her walking boots. Two bouncing dogs were excited to be going out again so soon and that made her smile. She had been smiling a lot over the last few days and it felt really good. Deciding to be really mindful during her walk, she took in everything. Every door colour, every garden, every turn, cracks in the pavements, every rock and most importantly every person she met. Saying hello to everyone on her trip was rewarding her with lots of smiles which was leaving her wanting more.

Today just "felt" different. There were goals and plans on her walls, some of them needed more substance but they were there. Making the long walk to the last beach, she reviewed the year in her head and thought about the anger that had been released just a few weeks ago. What became apparent was how much anger she had been holding back, which had impeded her in creating her way out from rock bottom. But, even as those words "rock bottom" entered her head, the feeling was that she was no longer there. How could rock bottom exist when she had her children, her dogs, enough money to live on, no debt and this beautiful location. It turned out that what had been visualised as a terrible place to be, compared to where she had been in her life, was not really a bad place after all. Thinking about her big salary and important job, other than the first ten years she couldn't remember feeling this happy, despite having all of that money. Her marriage certainly wasn't happy, not for a long time, maybe only the first two years. Her relationship with her sister had been toxic for possibly a decade because Angel was ill and Mandy now recognised that the only way to repair that relationship properly was to let her go, change the rules, and give it time for her sister to heal. The money that had been lost felt worthless and what did it buy? Only things. There were enough things to make life comfortable, so there was no rush to buy more.

Her thoughts had carried her past the beach they had explored for so long the previous day and onwards over dunes and sandy expanses dotted with grassy patches for about two miles, it had taken half an hour to get this far. Then the entry to beach four was visible, she attached the dogs leads as she needed to exit the dunes and take a short walk along the coastal road to the access point. It was like entering a cartoon. The dunes enveloped a small track rising around six feet on one side and ten on the other, it actually felt slightly enclosed. But it was a short path and emerging onto the beach she just stopped and took a sharp intake of breath. What had appeared to be the most beautiful beach she had ever seen yesterday, was nothing compared to this. This could be likened to a great masterpiece, immobilised and rooted to the spot she was taking it all in. To her right were miles of white sandy beach for as far as the eye could see, directly in front of her was that beautiful calm azure sea and to the left were rock pools and large rock structures to climb and sit on. Coquet Island nature reserve could be seen clearly with its white lighthouse to her left view, with the brilliant morning glory blue sky framing it like a watercolour painting.

Heading for the rocks to her left to sit she let the dogs off to run free. Once again, the only person on the beach with the exception of two distant dog walkers to her right, she felt blessed. Looking around once more she noticed the blue and white beach hut style houses with panoramic windows that framed this picture. *What a wonderful view to wake up to daily,* she thought.

Once again, her mind turned to this last month and how much relief she had experienced once she had decided to focus on forgiveness and gratitude. How could she not be grateful for this being on her doorstep? Knowing that her children had some healing to do yet felt like something that was manageable, she could be there for them and build her business slowly and steadily, after all, she had enough. Enough. That was all that was needed, for now, there was no need for fancy cars or diamonds and jewels, she had what she needed. A home, an income, her children, her family, friends and a plan. What more did anybody need? Living small and saving hard would be her next lesson and she was ready for it; she was prepared to be patient and not need any more than enough. The task would be to budget, plan and review. Her decision to say yes to every opportunity now had a caveat, say yes to everything that makes you and the children happy, if it didn't tick that box it wasn't going to happen.

The picture of emptiness had left her brain, replaced with smiling faces, full bellies and family days at the beach. Pictures of success and abundance were coming to her on a more frequent basis, wanting to paint them, but not quite being there yet was not even concerning her, she would write them for now and keep a record to use later. There were goals on every side of her perfect square, they were simple to start with; lose weight and get fit; start savings plans for the kids; work on self-love first and keep a constant visual of where they were going as a family. Simple but clear and she would expand and grow these goals on a path leading to their perfect home, however long that took. She would not falter or waiver on that path because once again there was confidence that she had the skills, the desire and nothing more to lose. What screamed at her at that moment was the realisation that as she had felt happier over the last few weeks, she had not even considered what her next challenge would be. That was progress. It had never even entered her head.

Looking around, taking in a deep breath of fresh sea air and acknowledging the feeling so that she could honour it, there was no worry.

This was huge. She was not worried at all; in fact, she was ready for absolutely anything that the universe wanted to throw at her. These last twelve months had taught her that even at her worst she had more skills than some people at their best, and that was a gift. How this gift was used would be part of the solution for her over the coming years. But for now, what she could feel in her very soul was that the challenges no longer mattered, she did not see them as challenges any longer, just life.

At that very moment, there was a chill breeze and a feeling that made Mandy turn her head towards her left. Sitting on the rock next to her was her dad. This time there was no hesitation in what to say.

'HI, Dad, I have missed you so much, you have left a massive gap.'

'I know, love, but it is now filled with knowledge. I knew that you would win because that is what I told you from the day you were born, you could do anything. I was right.'

'Thank you, Dad, for all that you gave me, and thank you for just being you. I will miss you, but I know you will always be here.'

She just knew that this moment could not be wasted.

'Stay strong, love, and you will always be a winner. I love you too.'

And with that, he was gone and Mandy knew that her blank page was there for her to write on. There were no tears, just love, gratitude and hope. And that felt good.